catch me

if you can

NO LONGER THE PROPERTY OF
BALDWIN PUBLIC LIBRARY

P9-CRQ-335

catch me

A STEVEN SPIELBERG FILM

if you can

**Introduction by
FRANK W. ABAGNALE**

Photographs by ANDREW COOPER

Screenplay by JEFF NATHANSON

**Based on the book by
FRANK W. ABAGNALE** with STAN REDDING

Edited by LINDA SUNSHINE

Designed by TIMOTHY SHANER

DREAMWORKS

A NEWMARKET PICTORIAL MOVIEBOOK

NEWMARKET PRESS • NEW YORK

TM & © 2002 DreamWorks. Cover art by BLT and Associates/David Sameth for DreamWorks SKG.

Quotes from *Catch Me If You Can* by Frank W. Abagnale with Stan Redding, © 1980 by Frank W. Abagnale. Used by permission of Broadway Books, a division of Random House. Cover on page 6: © 1977 Houston Chronicle Publishing Company. Reprinted with permission. All rights reserved. Quotes on page 13, 44 and 104 used by permission of Lewis Beale. Photo on page 19: "To Tell The Truth" is a trademark of FremantleMedia Operations BV. Used with kind permission.

All rights reserved. This book may not be reproduced, in whole or in part, in any form, without written permission. Inquiries should be addressed to Permissions Department, Newmarket Press, 18 East 48th Street, New York, NY 10017.

This book is published in the United States of America.

First Edition

10 9 8 7 6 5 4 3 2 1

Library of Congress Cataloging-in-Publication Data available upon request.

ISBN 1-55704-548-8 (Hardcover)
ISBN 1-55704-553-4 (Paperback)

QUANTITY PURCHASES
Companies, professional groups, clubs, and other organizations may qualify for special terms when ordering quantities of this title. For information, write Special Sales Department, Newmarket Press, 18 East 48th Street, New York, NY 10017; call (212) 832-3575; fax (212) 832-3629; or e-mail mailbox@newmarketpress.com.

www.newmarketpress.com

Design by Timothy Shaner.

Manufactured in the United States of America.

Other Newmarket Pictorial Moviebooks include:
Frida: Bringing Frida Kahlo's Life and Art to Film
E.T.: The Extra-Terrestrial From Concept to Classic
Windtalkers: The Making of the Film About the Navajo Code Talkers of World War II
Ali: The Movie and the Man
Planet of the Apes: Re-imagined by Tim Burton
Moulin Rouge: The Splendid Book that Charts the Journey of Baz Luhrmann's Motion Picture
The Art of The Matrix
Gladiator: The Making of the Ridley Scott Epic
Crouching Tiger, Hidden Dragon: A Portrait of the Ang Lee Film
Titus: The Illustrated Screenplay, Adapted from the Play by William Shakespeare
The Age of Innocence: A Portrait of the Film Based on the Novel by Edith Wharton
Cradle Will Rock: The Movie and the Moment
Dances With Wolves: The Illustrated Story of the Epic Film
Saving Private Ryan: The Men, the Mission, the Movie
Amistad: A Celebration of the Film by Steven Spielberg
Bram Stoker's Dracula: The Film and the Legend

contents

Introduction
by Frank W. Abagnale
7

The Cast
16

The Illustrated Screenplay
19

Credits
156

THIS MAN *LOOKS* LIKE AN AIRLINE PILOT, BUT THE TRUTH WILL ASTOUND YOU

Catch Me If You Can

BY FRANK W. ABAGNALE

Catch Me If You Can took a very long, circuitous route through Hollywood to eventually land with Steven Spielberg. It's a long story; let me start at the beginning.

The rights to the movie were sold before the book was written. In 1977, I appeared on the *Today Show with Tom Brokaw*, and, soon after, received a phone call from the people at the *Tonight Show with Johnny Carson*. Mr. Carson had seen me on *The Today Show* and wanted me to be a guest on his program. I was happy to oblige, of course, though I was a bit perplexed about what we could discuss since I did not have a book to promote. The producer explained that Mr. Carson wanted to talk about my past life and what I currently did during a six-minute segment of the show. Well, my six-minute appearance turned into a twenty-minute segment. After the show, several hundred people called, asking where they could buy my book. Of course, there wasn't a book at that time, although I wrote *Catch Me If You Can* shortly thereafter.

Soon after I was contacted about selling my story to the movies. In 1978, I entered into an agreement with Bud Yorkin. We signed an option contract that would be the model for all the contracts to follow. After two years Mr. Yorkin said, "Frank, I am not going to

LEFT: *Frank W. Abagnale on the cover of a Houston magazine in 1977.* RIGHT: *Abagnale on location with* Catch Me If You Can, *2002.*

be able to do this film, but someday someone is going to make it, and it's going to be big." Over the next few years, the rights for the film were optioned to Columbia TV and then to Grosso-Jacobson Productions. In 1986, Hall Bartlett came forward and optioned the film, an option they held for the next four years. During this time a number of scripts were written, but none of them were acceptable. Several actors were considered to play my character—Tom Cruise, Eddie Murphy, and David Hasselhoff, among others.

By then I had decided that if Mr. Bartlett was not going to purchase the film, the rights should revert back to me. Much to my surprise he paid the full purchase price of $250,000 for the rights to the film. From this point on, I would never see another cent from the rights to *Catch Me If You Can*, nor would I have any control over what became of the film.

> I would say that 90 percent of the film is accurate. The movie is based on my life but it's not a documentary. Jeff Nathanson, the screenwriter, took everything into consideration and then condensed five years of my life into a two-hour movie. Obviously, he had to take some shortcuts and change some things, but I think the movie really captures my essence of the story.
> —Frank W. Abagnale, on the movie

In 1990, Michel Shane, an independent film producer, called to inquire about the film rights. He was directed to Mr. Bartlett who sold the rights to him for $300,000. He, in turn, optioned the film to Hollywood Pictures, a division of Disney, who held onto the project for two years and then reverted the rights back to Mr. Shane. The project sat around for some time while numerous people considered the idea, including the Coen brothers. Then, in the fall of 1994, Sony Tri-Star optioned the film and held the rights for one year. Two years later, Barry Kemp and Bungalow 78 Productions optioned the book with an eye to developing the film. Finally, Mr. Kemp and his associate, Devorah Moos-Hankin, brought the project to producers Walter Parkes and Laurie MacDonald at DreamWorks.

By this time I had begun to lose interest in the film altogether. It had passed hands so many times, and had been "in the works" for so long that I did not think it would ever be made. Quite frankly, it didn't matter to me one way or the other. When I was younger it seemed cool and fun to have a movie made about

my youth, but as I became older such vanity and egotism had faded. Generally speaking, my past is not something I care to revisit, and I hesitate to see it glamorized in any way. So, when I heard that DreamWorks was interested in optioning it, I just saw it as one more company to take on the film. One more studio that would hold onto it and then let it go several years later.

This impression initially seemed justified because it was in development at DreamWorks for a couple years. However, there was a lot of behind-the-scenes activity and commitment occurring. As it turns out, DreamWorks had to start from scratch in an effort to shape and redefine the project. Jeff Nathanson, who had a prior association with Walter Parkes and Laurie MacDonald, as well as Ms. Moos-Hankin, went to work on a new screenplay. Two years and several drafts later, it was Jeff's script highlighting the father-son relationship that began to attract some high profile actors and directors.

When Leonardo DiCaprio agreed to do the film fairly early on, the process sped up notably. Mr. DiCaprio, thankfully, was interested in making a film that captured an accurate portrayal of my character at that time in my life. It was during this time that Steven Spielberg became interested in *Catch Me*. After a meeting with Parkes and MacDonald, Mr. Spielberg took the script Nathanson had penned and had his wife and children read the script and act out certain scenes. He said that while considering making the film, it was as if someone came up, tapped him on the shoulder and said, "You need to make this film." Mr. Spielberg decided to make the film with Leonardo DiCaprio.

At this point, I once again became interested in the film because the players involved seemed so genuinely dedicated, beginning with

LEFT: *Frank W. Abagnale wasn't yet out of his teens when this photo was taken of him as he impersonated a Pan Am pilot.* ABOVE LEFT: *Abagnale impersonating a doctor in a hospital in Atlanta.* ABOVE RIGHT: *Here he is photographed pretending to be a lawyer in Louisiana. The pictures on these pages are from Abagnale's personal archive. Understandably, he did not like to be photographed during this period of his life.*

8 734
ATLANTA

Jeff Nathanson and the producers. Initially I played no part in the workings of the film, and I was more than fine with that. However, when pre-production for the film began Mr. DiCaprio requested a phone interview with me. Of course I agreed, and one night we began discussing who I was then, and who I've since become.

From very early on, I was impressed with Leonardo. He is very articulate, honest and sincere. Soon after this phone conversation he asked if I would visit him at his home for a couple of days. I agreed and looked forward to meeting him in person. We had a wonderful rapport. I found his questions to be well crafted and thoughtful, showing a genuine desire to play my character with integrity and accuracy. He asked me about my habits, my feelings, and any mannerisms I had then or may have now. By the time our visit ended, I felt that I could not have asked for more in an actor, and a person, to play me than Leonardo.

The former police chief of Houston once said of me: "Frank Abagnale could write a check on toilet paper drawn on the Confederate States Treasury, sign it 'U.R. Hooked' and cash it at any bank in town, using a Hong Kong driver's license for identification."
—FRANK W. ABAGNALE, *CATCH ME IF YOU CAN*, WITH STAN REDDING, 1980

I would discover the same to be true about Tom Hanks and Steven Spielberg regarding their respective roles in bringing the film to life. I met Tom Hanks at an FBI lecture I gave. He was not only very funny, but also very genuine. He had read both of my books and enjoyed them very much. I was becoming more and more pleased with the way the movie was panning out.

Soon after, I met with Steven Spielberg for lunch one afternoon in Los Angeles. I expected a rushed meeting and a lecture on how the movie would be made. Instead, I found myself doing most of the talking, telling Steven many of the things I am relating now. We had a wonderful meeting. I found Steven to be very down to earth,

LEFT: *Leonardo DiCaprio in a scene from the movie where he is captured and put in prison.* ABOVE: *The real Frank W. Abagnale photographed during his stint as a professor of sociology at a college in Salt Lake City, Utah. Due to time constraints, this time period in Frank's life could not be included in the movie.*

compassionate, and kind. Many of my concerns regarding the film were addressed, and I expressed my understanding that this is a film, one meant to entertain. I understood, and understand, that it is not a documentary about this brief time in my life.

I visited the set a couple of times during the filming of the movie and I was always impressed. Everyone was professional and their attention to detail was remarkable. I had the pleasure of meeting Christopher Walken and watching him act in several scenes—which made my three sons very jealous. The experience further reinforced my belief that a truly incredible group of professionals had come together to make this movie. It was this belief that convinced me, at Mr. Spielberg's request, to appear in a cameo for the film. I enjoyed going to work with such talented people as much as I enjoyed meeting them.

Upon reflection, my feelings regarding the movie are quite simple. I see the movie as an interpretation of a mere fifth of my life, based on a book I wrote more than twenty years ago. The film is meant to entertain by conveying a sense of that era in history and one person's

BELOW: *Frank W. Abagnale with his wife and three sons in Montreal, Canada during the shooting of the scenes that take place in France. Abagnale plays a cameo role as a French policeman, as seen on page 141.*

unique journey through it. I do not see the film as biographical, even though it is accurate in many respects, and the scams and cons are all my own. Instead, I view it as a story based on my life, a story that takes certain liberties to make an entertaining and coherent two-hour film. I would not expect, nor perhaps would I even want, a completely detailed biographical account of my years on the run to be summed up in a movie. After all, it was only a short period in my life and could never, no matter how it was told, reveal the whole story.

It has been a long journey for this film — from the time I sold the rights to when it was finally made by Steven Spielberg and his talented cast and crew.

It was well worth the wait.

> This story could only have taken place in an age of innocence, which we are no longer about as a global community. Today people are generally more suspicious of each other, whereas in the sixties there was a community of trust. That innocence was something all of us are nostalgic about.
> —STEVEN SPIELBERG

ABOVE: *Leonardo DiCaprio and Frank W. Abagnale on location. Abagnale spent several days with the actor before shooting began and served as consultant on the film.*

CHECK FRAUD

the illustrated > screenplay

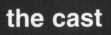

the cast

TOM HANKS as Carl Hanratty

LEONARDO DICAPRIO as Frank Abagnale Jr.

CHRISTOPHER WALKEN as Frank Abagnale Sr.

NATHALIE BAYE as Paula Abagnale

MARTIN SHEEN as Roger Strong

AMY ADAMS as Bronda Strong

JENNIFER GARNER as Cheryl Ann

INT. - GAME SHOW SET. - DAY
COLOR FOOTAGE FROM 1978

MUSIC UP:

A simple GAME SHOW SET — one long desk that houses four "CELEBRITY PANELISTS," a small pulpit with attached microphone for the host.

> **ANNOUNCER**
> Ladies and Gentleman, from New York City, it's Joe Garagiola.

JOE GARAGIOLA walks through the curtain to the delight of the audience.

> **JOE GARAGIOLA**
> Thank you very much and welcome to "To Tell the Truth." Now, if you're a faithful viewer of this show, you know that this game is played with one real person who must always tell the truth, right, and then two impostors who can lie right through their teeth, okay. Well our first guest, he's made a career out of being the most outrageous impostor that we've ever come across on this show, and you're going to see what I mean right after we meet our panel. Our regulars, Cass, Cullen, and Carlisle. And now this week we got the very real Nipsey Russell.

> **NIPSEY RUSSELL**
> Indeed.

> **JOE GARAGIOLA**
> And with that, let's meet a champion impostor.

Curtains open and THREE MEN walk onto the stage.

> **ANNOUNCER**
> Number one, what is your name please?

> **NUMBER 1**
> My name is Frank Abagnale Jr.

> **ANNOUNCER**
> Number two.

> **NUMBER 2**
> My name is Frank Abagnale Jr.

> **ANNOUNCER**
> And Number three.

> **NUMBER 3**
> My name is Frank Abagnale Jr.

> **JOE GARAGIOLA**
> Don't miss a word of the various life stories of Frank William Abagnale.

Camera cuts to the THREE FRANKS. Push in on FRANK NUMBER 1, then PAN across the other TWO FRANKS during Joe Garagiola's V.O.

> **JOE GARAGIOLA**
> My name is Frank Abagnale Jr., and some people consider me the world's greatest impostor. And no wonder. From 1964 to 1967, I successfully impersonated an airline pilot for Pan Am Airlines, and flew over two million miles for free. During that time I was also the

ABOVE: *Frank W. Abagnale, as he appeared on the television show "To Tell The Truth" in the late 1970s.*

Chief Resident Pediatrician at a Georgia hospital and the Assistant Attorney General for the state of Louisiana. By the time I was caught and sentenced to prison, I had cashed almost four million dollars in fraudulent checks in 26 foreign countries and all fifty states, and I did it all before my 19th birthday. My name is Frank Abagnale Jr.

The three contestants walk to their seats.

JOE GARAGIOLA
So for the first time he's gonna have to tell the truth and we're gonna start our questions with Kitty.

KITTY CARLISLE
Thank you. Well, whoever you are, I don't think you're exactly to be congratulated, but it is a marvelous story. Number one, how many years were you in prison?

NUMBER 1
I served two years in France, and four years in Atlanta, Georgia.

KITTY CARLISLE
Oh, I see. Number two, I find all this very fascinating. Who was it that finally caught you?

SLOWLY PUSH IN ON THE PILOT IN THE MIDDLE — A thin smile across his lips as he faces the panel — his manicured hands out in front of him on the desk — his back straight in his chair — his cap pulled slightly forward on his head — the way pilots like to wear them.

EXT. - PERPIGNAN MAXIMUM SECURITY PRISON. - FRANCE. - DAY
SUPER: FRANCE, CHRISTMAS EVE, 1969

SECURITY GUARD
Han-rat-tay.

HANRATTY
Hanratty. Carl Hanratty.

A heavy rain falls on CARL HANRATTY, 40s, who wears a black hat and holds a black umbrella as he bangs on the window of a small GUARD SHACK in front of a LARGE GATED PRISON. Carl is sneezing as he holds up an IDENTIFICATION CARD TO THE GUARD.

HANRATTY
FBI.

INT. - PERPIGNAN PRISON. - DAY
Carl is walking down a long corridor inside the prison, struggling to close his umbrella as he faces WARDEN GARREN and TWO GUARDS.

HANRATTY
I have orders to see a prisoner named Abagnale, to witness his statement and certify his rights, so I can prepare for tomorrow's extradition.

The Warden stares at Hanratty, takes the umbrella from him and casually closes it. He hands it back to Carl.

HANRATTY
I also have a little cold. You guys think you could turn up the heat in here?

INT. - PERPIGNAN PRISON. - DAY
WARDEN GARREN is leading Carl down a long, isolated corridor just off the main floor of the prison. They pass CEMENT

Oddly enough, I never felt like a criminal. I was one, of course, and I was aware of the fact. I've been described by the authorities and news reporters as one of this century's cleverest bum-check passers, flimflam artists and crooks, a con man of Academy Award caliber. I was a swindler and poseur of astonishing ability. I sometimes astonished myself with some of my impersonations and shenanigans, but I never at any time deluded myself. I was always aware that I was Frank Abagnale, Jr., that I was a check swindler and a faker, and if and when I was caught I wasn't going to win any Oscars. I was going to jail.

—Frank W. Abagnale, from his book

DOORS with metal SLIDE HOLES and numbers taped to the front. There are no bars or windows in this area, and complete silence. Garren stops at the last cell and opens the SLIDE HOLE.

> **WARDEN GARREN**
> Sit here. Don't cross the line. Don't pass him anything through the hole.

Garren walks off, and Carl looks uneasy as he stares at the cell door. Carl gets out of the chair, crosses the line, and kneels down to look through the metal slide hole.

> **HANRATTY**
> Jesus, Frank, I heard about French prisons, but this...

THROUGH THE HOLE WE SEE FRANK ABAGNALE JR., his face hidden in the dim cell, which gets its only light from a hanging bulb. Frank's eyes are closed, and he's lying awkwardly on the cement floor with his back against the far wall. He wears only a pair of underwear and has a torn blanket clutched in his hand. SILENCE from the cell as Carl takes a step back, finds his chair. He takes out a thick stack of legal papers.

> **HANRATTY**
> I'm going to read you the Articles of Extradition as established by the European Court of Human Rights.
> (*starts to read*)
> Article one states that extradition shall be granted in respect to offenses punishable...

Carl stops reading, listens for a BEAT.

> **HANRATTY**
> You with me on this, Frank? Don't go to sleep on me now. We have 16 pages to get through.

Carl gets out of the chair, starts to whisper through the slot.

> **HANRATTY**
> Frank, I know you can hear me. Come on, Frank, we have work to do.

Carl reaches into the cell with his umbrella, taps Frank on the shoulder.

INSIDE THE CELL
FRANK'S BODY SLOWLY SLIDES OFF THE WALL — falling into the light — his head hitting the cement.

CLOSE ON FRANK ABAGNALE JR. — lying dead in his cell — his face covered by a beard and matted black hair. His eyes closed and mouth open — body lifeless — blood flowing from his head onto the floor and into the light.

Carl stares in at Frank, quickly pulls in his umbrella.

> **HANRATTY**
> Frank? Damn it, Frank, stop this right now. Do you hear me — I know you can hear me!

Carl starts to read from his papers.

I had no idea what Frank Abagnale was going to be like before I met him. Of course, he's a dapper, well dressed, and incredibly well-presented man. He exudes a brand of confidence I wish I had. I attended a seminar he presented to a group of bank security experts and law enforcement people. It could have been a one-man show on Broadway. I've since read his book and have regaled people at dinner parties over and over again with this or that scam of his.

Meeting Frank actually empowered my work as Carl Hanratty. After seeing what a smart, confident, and charismatic man he is, I could better understand the relationship in the movie between Carl and Frank — which mirrors the real life relationship between the real Carl and Frank.

I have a lot of respect for this guy who embezzled millions of dollars and forged all kinds of checks. Carl Hanratty has the same kind of respect.

—Tom Hanks

The French prisons are very strict. It was very hard when I was in there. I was so mad. Now that I've gotten older, I believe that the French probably have the best prison system in the world. Here in America we have two million people in prison. We're paying $25,000 a year to house an inmate. They're living in air conditioning. They have miniature golf, tennis courts and swimming pools. The rate of recidivism in this country is that about 68 percent of all criminals go back to prison within six months.

Now, people say the French prisons are harsh and they are. They spend less than $1,000 a year to house an inmate though the sentences are much shorter.

After a prisoner is released, they have less than a half a percent ever returning to prison.

Obviously, the reality is the French prison system works better than ours. Although I'm not into mistreating prisoners or beating them, I do think the French concept is that you go to prison to be punished, not to live a better life than you lived on the streets. I really don't have a lot of grudges against the French prison system anymore.

—Frank W. Abagnale, on the movie

      HANRATTY
Article two. Extradition shall not be granted if the offense in respect to which it is requested...

Carl looks up from his papers, sees Frank lying on the cell floor. He stares at him for a BEAT, searching for any sign of life.

      HANRATTY
Goddamn it, just calm down, you're okay. Do you hear me, stop this shit right now!

Carl steps away from the door — yells down the empty hallway.

      HANRATTY
I need someone to open this door. Do you people hear me, I represent the United States government and I am asking for medical attention! You are not gonna take this from me! My prisoner is not going to bleed to death in that cell tonight!

SMASH CUT:

THE CELL DOOR IS THROWN OPEN

Frank is being dragged across the floor by Warden Garren and a second GUARD, each holding an arm as they drag Frank's emaciated six-foot frame through the halls. Carl Hanratty jogs behind the guards, following the trail of Frank's blood.

      HANRATTY
Just wake up and open your eyes, Frank! Where's the doctor? Where are you taking him?

INT. - PERPIGNAN PRISON INFIRMARY. - DAY
A small, empty room with four empty hospital beds. Frank is thrown

onto one of the beds, his legs flailing out to the sides, catching on a thin curtain which pulls out from the wall.

HANRATTY
I don't think he's breathing. Where's the doctor? Frank, wake up, Frank!

Garren and the Guard quickly move toward a sink, where they start to wash their hands.

HANRATTY
What are you doing?

WARDEN GARREN
Washing off the lice.

HANRATTY
You have to call a doctor right now. In 24 hours, I'm putting this man on a plane!

WARDEN GARREN
The doctor comes tomorrow.

HANRATTY
You are not gonna let him die. I have orders from the American Embassy, and I am holding you responsible if anything...

Suddenly Garren looks past Hanratty — eyeing the curtain that partially encloses Frank's bed. Garren slowly moves toward the curtain, pushes it open.

FRANK IS GONE

CLOSE ON: GARREN drawing his gun and sprinting out the open door of the infirmary, yelling in French for the Guard to follow. Carl Hanratty stands motionless, staring down in horror at the empty bed.

HANRATTY
Oh, shit...Frank!

INT. - PRISON. - CONTINUOUS
The prison ALARM has sent every prisoner to the front of their cells, where they see Frank stumbling through the prison — a thin smile on his lips as he tries to move his starved legs toward the main door. As Frank makes his way past a row of cheering prisoners, he trips and falls, his body too weak to run as he starts to crawl across the prison floor.

Carl and Garren easily catch up to him, Garren quickly kneeling down and holding his gun against Frank's head — cocking the weapon. Frank stops crawling, rolls over on his back, and smiles up at Carl Hanratty.

FRANK
Okay, Carl...let's go home.

INT. - NEW ROCHELLE ROTARY CLUB. - BANQUET ROOM. - NIGHT
SUPER: NEW ROCHELLE, NEW YORK, 1963

The sound of APPLAUSE washes over a smoke filled oak dining room packed with CLUB MEMBERS — HUNDREDS OF MIDDLE-AGED WHITE MEN wearing black suits and holding long cigars as they drink from brandy glasses.

FRANK ABAGNALE, 15, wearing a WESTBOURNE PRIVATE SCHOOL BLUE BLAZER, THIN BLACK TIE, AND WHITE PANTS, sits with his mother, PAULA, 33, at a center table near the stage. Paula is a stunning blonde dressed in diamonds and fur, and since she's the only woman in the room — she's getting a lot of attention. Frank is carefully PEELING THE LABEL off a wine bottle that sits in front of him.

CLUB PRESIDENT JACK BARNES takes the microphone at the front of the stage.

JACK BARNES
The New Rochelle Rotary Club has a history that goes back to 1919. In all those years, we have only inducted a handful of deserving men as lifetime members, an honor that has seen 57 names enshrined on the wall of honor. Tonight, we make it 58. So please stand, as I present my good friend, a man who keeps our pencils sharp and our pens in ink — Frank William Abagnale.

Applause all around as FRANK ABAGNALE SR. steps up to the MICROPHONE. He is handsome and impeccably groomed — wearing a black suit and holding onto his plaque with two hands.

FRANK SR.
Two little mice fell in a bucket of cream. The first mouse quickly gave up and drowned, but the second mouse wouldn't quit. He struggled so hard, that he eventually churned that cream into butter — and crawled out. Gentleman, as of this moment, I am that second mouse.

Laughter from the men in the room as Frank continues.

FRANK SR.
I stand here today humbled by the presence of Mayor Robert Wagner, and our club president, Jack Barnes. But most of all, I am honored to see my loving wife, Paula, and my son, Frank Jr., sitting in the front row. I'm just a business man, a working stiff — but tonight you have made me royalty. And for this, I am eternally grateful.

The men applaud as Frank Sr. smiles down at his wife and son, giving them a wink as he raises the plaque in the air.

EXT. - FRANK'S HOUSE. - NEW ROCHELLE. - DAY
A tree-lined, picturesque slice of suburbia, with Cadillacs in the driveways and kids playing in the street.

INT. - FRANK'S HOUSE. - DAY
DEAN MARTIN is singing EVERYBODY LOVES SOMEBODY on the radio, as Frank Sr. hammers his PLAQUE into the wall. In the middle of the DEN, Frank is dancing with his mother, who is holding a glass of wine as she dances.

PAULA
You're a better dancer than your father, Frankie. The girls don't know what they're in for.

FRANK SR.
Paula, show him the dance you were doing when we met.

PAULA
Who can remember?

FRANK SR.
The people in that little village were so happy to see Americans, that they decided to put on a show for us.

FRANK
I know the story, Daddy.

FRANK SR.
So they cram two hundred soldiers into this tiny social hall, and the first person to walk on stage is your mother. And she starts to dance...

Paula steps away from Frank, and she starts to dance a ballet, smiling as she tries to remember the steps.

FRANK SR.
It had been months since we had even seen a woman, and here's this blonde angel on stage — and the men are literally holding their breath. And I turned to my buddies, and I said...

FRANK
(*imitating his father*)
I will not leave France without her.

FRANK SR.
And I didn't. I didn't.

Paula spins around, accidently SPILLS HER GLASS OF WINE —

PAULA
Oh, shit, the rug! I can't believe I did that. Frankie, run and
get a towel....

As Frank runs off, Paula drops to her knees and scrubs the stain with
the hem of her dress.

PAULA
This will never come out.

She looks up at her husband.

PAULA
Whenever I dance for you, I get in trouble.

INT. - FRANK'S BEDROOM. - MORNING
Frank is asleep in his bedroom, a copy of THE FLASH comic book lying
by his side. His father walks in carrying a plate of scrambled eggs.

FRANK SR.
Wake up, Frank... it's 8:30.

Frank opens his eyes, stares at his father.

FRANK
I overslept. Mom's gonna kill me.

FRANK SR.
It's okay, I let you sleep. You don't have to go to school today.

FRANK
Is it snowing?

FRANK SR.
We have a very important meeting in the city.

EXT. - MEN'S SHOP. - NEW ROCHELLE. - MORNING
THE WHITE CADILLAC is parked in front of A MEN'S CLOTHING
STORE — Frank Sr. banging on the glass door, trying to get someone's
attention.

FRANK SR.
Ma'am, open the door. Just open up, please, it's important.

THE DOOR OPENS A CRACK AND DARCY, 40s, low-cut blouse, a
bagel in her hand, stares at Frank Sr.

DARCY
We don't open for half an hour.

FRANK SR.
What's your name, ma'am?

DARCY
Darcy.

FRANK SR.
Darcy, that's a pretty name. I'm in a bit of fix — I need a
suit for my kid. This is my son, Frank, he needs a black suit.
There was a death in the family, my father, 85 years old, a
war hero, there's a funeral this afternoon — a military funeral —
planes flying overhead, 21 gun salute. Frank needs to borrow
a suit for a couple of hours.

DARCY
I'm sorry. We don't loan suits, and we're not open.

As she closes the door, Frank Sr. takes a small GOLD NECKLACE
OUT OF HIS POCKET, holds it up to the glass.

FRANK SR.
Is this yours, Darcy? I just found it in the parking lot.

Darcy stares at the necklace through the door.

FRANK SR.
Must have slipped right off your neck.

EXT. - NEW YORK CITY. - DAY
The Cadillac is parked somewhere in MANHATTAN.

Frank, now wearing a BLACK SUIT and black hat, watches as his
father gets out of the car and climbs into the back seat.

FRANK SR.
Slide over. You're gonna take me up to Chase Manhattan Bank. Just
pull up to the front and park next to the fire hydrant.

Frank looks back at his father.

FRANK
Dad...I don't know how to drive.

FRANK SR.
We're only going a hundred feet. I'll talk you through it.

Frank slides over, nervously puts his hands on the wheel.

FRANK SR.
Just pump the gas — now put it in drive and slowly press the pedal.
That's good, easy now — a little more — now stay against the curb
— slowly!

THE CADILLAC SWERVES INTO THE CURB — THEN BACK

Pointy Bras

All the women in the movie, even extras in the background, had to wear period authentic foundations. These have conical-shaped cups which give a pointed silhouette. Nobody went without one of those bras during that time so it was very important to me that we capture those kinds of details. It is the layering in of this kind of detail that is essential to setting an accurate tone and really transporting the actors and audience to that time and place. Also the appropriate bra makes the authentic period clothing we used fit properly. We could not cast women with breast implants because they do not fit into that pointy silhouette.

—MARY ZOPHRES, COSTUME DESIGNER

Hairstyles

Hairstyle has the ability to instantly put you in a particular period so we did demand authenticity on this front. During the time period of the movie, women went to the beauty parlor and had a very groomed, coiffed look (even the younger women). Men, conversely, went to the barbershop where their specific cut and sideburns were maintained. We kept the look focused in the early 1960s.

When time passed in the movie to 1966, Frank was in the slower-paced south where our research showed that people were not sporting the latest fashion or hairstyles.

Early on, Steven Spielberg made it clear that he didn't want the movie to be about capturing each year with a change in style. I think there is a real innocence to the look of the early 1960s, an innocence in which this story should be told.

When the movie moves to 1968 we are in a small rural town in the south of France. Here, we backdated the look even further and gave it a real rustic quality. The men have more facial hair, the older women have hairstyles from the 1950s or some have long hair in buns or up in kerchiefs. It's a subtle difference that that will indicate to the moviegoer that Frank is in a very different environment.

Our brief move to the 1970s is also very subtle, both in clothing and in hair. It is there, but in very subtle ways.

—MARY ZOPHRES, COSTUME DESIGNER

TOWARD TRAFFIC — ALMOST HITTING A CAB — CARS HONK-
ING AND SLAMMING ON THEIR BRAKES AS FRANK SR. STICKS
HIS HEAD OUT THE WINDOW.

> **FRANK SR.**
> (*yelling out the window*)
> Don't honk at us you son of a bitch — I'm teaching my kid to drive!
> You're doing fine, Frank, keep it straight now — almost there —
> watch the curb!

The car slams into the curb — rims scraping as Frank almost hits several trash cans, then finally straightens the wheel.

> **FRANK SR.**
> Perfect! Now you got it! Look at you, Frank, this is your
> town — you're going straight up 40th and Park!

INT. - CHASE MANHATTAN. - DAY
EMPLOYEES ARE HELPING CUSTOMERS in the hushed silence of
the MASSIVE BANK. Suddenly all eyes turn to the street, where A
WHITE CADILLAC SPEEDS TO A STOP IN FRONT OF THE GLASS
DOORS. A CHAUFFEUR IN A BLACK SUIT AND HAT IS OPENING
THE BACK DOOR OF THE CAR, WHICH IS PARKED NEXT TO A
FIRE HYDRANT.

EXT. - CHASE MANHATTAN BANK. - DAY
Frank Sr. steps out of the Cadillac, gives his son a wink.

> **FRANK SR.**
> Okay. Stop grinning. When I get inside you go back to the front seat
> and wait. Even if a cop comes and writes you a ticket, you don't
> move the car, understood?

> **FRANK**
> Dad...is this really gonna help?

> **FRANK SR.**
> You know why the Yankees always win, Frank?

> **FRANK**
> They have Mickey Mantle?

> **FRANK SR.**
> No. It's because the other teams can't stop staring at those damn
> pinstripes.

Frank Sr. grabs his briefcase.

> **FRANK SR.**
> Watch this, Frank. The manager of Chase Manhattan bank is about
> to open the door for your father.

As Frank Sr. casually walks toward the doors of Chase Manhattan, the
MANAGER rushes through the bank to open the doors for him.

INT. - LOAN DEPARTMENT. - CHASE MANHATTAN BANK. - DAY
Frank Sr. is sitting across from a LOAN OFFICER, who is looking over
his file.

> **LOAN OFFICER**
> Mr. Abagnale, we don't usually loan money to people who have
> unresolved business with the IRS

> **FRANK SR.**
> That's just a misunderstanding. I hired the wrong guy to do my
> books, a mistake anyone could make. I just need you guys to help
> me weather the storm.

> **LOAN OFFICER**
> Sir, you're being investigated by the government for tax fraud.

FRANK SR.
My store is a landmark in New Rochelle. I have customers all over
New York.

LOAN OFFICER
You're not a customer of Chase Manhattan. We don't know you. I'm
sure your bank in New Rochelle...

FRANK SR.
My bank went out of business. Banks like this put them out of
business.

Frank Sr. leans in, lowers his voice.

FRANK SR.
Now I know I made a mistake, I admit that. But these people want
blood — they want my store — they've threatened to put me in jail.
This is America, right, I'm not a criminal. I'm a medal of honor
winner, a lifetime member of the New Rochelle Rotary Club. All I'm
asking you to do is help me beat these guys.

LOAN OFFICER
This is not a question of winning and losing. It's a question of risk.

FRANK SR.
You're the largest bank in the world. Where's the fucking risk?

EXT. - CHASE MANHATTAN BANK. - DAY
Frank is anxiously waiting for his father in front of the bank. He looks
behind him, sees two more LIMO DRIVERS in dark suits and black
hats, both waiting for their "clients." Frank catches his own reflection
in the car window — pulls his hat slightly forward.

EXT. - USED CAR LOT. - DAY
A SALESMAN is handing Frank Sr. A CHECK and a set of KEYS.
Frank and his father glance toward an OLD, DENTED CHEVY
IMPALA at the back of the lot.

THE SALESMAN gets in the CADILLAC and drives it toward the
front of the car lot.

FRANK
Dad, you can't just let him take our car.

FRANK SR.
He didn't take anything. We took him. He overpaid by five hundred.

Frank Sr. smiles as he shows his son the CHECK in his hand.

FRANK SR.
Come on, son. Let's go return the suit.

EXT. - FRANK'S HOUSE. - DAY
A MOVING TRUCK IS DRIVING AWAY FROM THE HOUSE. The
Chevy Impala is packed with boxes as it slowly pulls out of the
driveway, passing the SOLD SIGN on the front lawn as it follows
the moving truck through the neighborhood.

EXT. - EASTCHESTER TRAIN STATION. - SUNSET
A CARGO TRAIN pulls into a run-down station that is flanked by
dilapidated APARTMENT BUILDINGS AND TENEMENT HOUSES.

INT. - EASTCHESTER APARTMENT. - SUNSET
A TWO BEDROOM APARTMENT with cracks in the ceiling that
seem to grow with each passing train. There are MOVING BOXES
STACKED AGAINST THE WALLS and a dining room table that
seems to take up half the apartment. All of the old furniture seems
large and out of place in the new apartment.

Frank is in the kitchen making dinner as his father walks in from
work — his suit wrinkled, his briefcase in hand.

FRANK SR.
Where's your mother?

FRANK
She said she was going to look for a job.

Frank Sr. laughs, and after a BEAT Frank laughs with him.

I play Frank's father.

We're close. I guess you could say that I encourage him in his pursuits. I'm a little bit of a crook myself.
—Christopher Walken

FRANK
I'm making pancakes and eggs.

FRANK SR.
We're not gonna eat pancakes for dinner on my son's sixteenth birthday.

Frank turns to his father.

FRANK SR.
Why are you looking at me like that? You thought I forgot?

Frank opens his BRIEFCASE, takes out a CHECKBOOK FROM CHASE MANHATTAN BANK. He walks over and hands it to Frank.

FRANK SR.
I opened a checking account in your name. I put twenty-five dollars in the account so you can buy whatever you want. Don't tell your mother.

Frank slowly opens the CHECKBOOK, sees his name at the top of the first check.

FRANK
But they turned down your loan?

FRANK SR.
Yeah. They all turned me down.

FRANK
So why open a bank account with them?

FRANK SR.
Because one day you'll want something from these people —
a house, a car — they have all the money. There's a hundred
checks here, Frank, which means from this day on — you're in
their little club.

EXT. - BELLARMINE JEFFERSON HIGH SCHOOL. - MORNING
THE IMPALA pulls up to the front of the local public High School.
Frank wears his BLUE BLAZER AND WHITE PANTS as he gets out of
the car and smiles at his mother. Paula wears an OLD FUR COAT over
her pajamas.

PAULA
See that, it's just a school. No different than Westbourne.

Frank reaches through the window of the car, takes the CIGARETTE
out of his mother's mouth.

FRANK
You promised you were going to quit.

PAULA
Frankie, you don't have to wear the uniform here. Why don't you
take the jacket off?

FRANK
I'm used to it.

INT. - BELLARMINE JEFFERSON HIGH SCHOOL. - DAY
Frank walks through the crowded halls looking lost as he holds a
CLASS SCHEDULE. A swarm of kids rush past him, and Frank tries
to get the attention of a cute CHEERLEADER.

FRANK
Excuse me, I'm looking for room 17, French...

A BIG KID IN A LETTERMAN'S JACKET deliberately bumps him
and Frank loses his balance and slams against a locker. As several kids
laugh, Frank adjusts his tie and continues through the halls.

INT. - CLASSROOM. - DAY
Frank walks into a packed, raucous classroom, the STUDENTS turning
to stare as he checks his schedule.

STUDENT #1
You selling encyclopedias?

Scattered laughter from the kids. The big kid in the Letterman's jacket
takes a seat in the front row.

FOOTBALL PLAYER
He looks like the sub?

More laughter as the kids turn back to their friends. Frank nervously
adjusts his tie, sees that there is no teacher. He walks toward the front
of the room, then SLAMS THE BACK OF AN ERASER AGAINST
THE BLACKBOARD to get the students attention.

The entire class stares up at Frank, who starts to write his name on the
board. Frank finishes writing his name, then calmly turns to the class.

FRANK
Quiet down, people. My name is Mr. Abagnale and I'll be your substitute today. Would somebody please tell me where you left
off in your text book?

Dead silence for a BEAT as the kids stare at Frank.

FRANK
If I have to ask again I'm gonna write up the entire class.

GIRL #1
Chapter seven.

FRANK
Open your books to chapter eight and we'll get started.
(*to the football player*)
Why don't you come up here and read conversation number five.

The football player looks petrified as the classroom door swings open, and a frail, confused TEACHER walks in and motions to Frank.

TEACHER
They sent for me — they said they needed a sub for Roberta.
I came all the way from Dixon.

FRANK
I always sub for Roberta. Why aren't you reading!

The football player tries to read a few words, and everyone starts to laugh at him.

TEACHER
I'll never come to Bellarmine Jefferson again. You tell them
not to call me!

The WOMAN storms out, and Frank turns back to the football player and smiles.

FRANK
Louder.

INT. - PRINCIPAL'S OFFICE. - BELLARMINE JEFFERSON HIGH SCHOOL. - DAY
CLOSE ON: A SILVER ZIPPO LIGHTING A CIGARETTE —PRINCIPAL EVANS is standing in front of Frank Sr. and Paula, who sit in two small chairs facing him. Paula sets the lighter back on the Principal's desk as she begins to smoke.

PAULA
I'm not sure I understand. Has Frank been coming to school or not?

PRINCIPAL EVANS
Mr. and Mrs. Abagnale, this is not a question of your son's atten-dance. I regret to inform you that for the past week, Frank has been teaching Ms. Glasser's French class.

PAULA
He what?

PRINCIPAL EVANS
Your son has been pretending to be a substitute teacher, lecturing the students, giving out homework. Mrs. Glasser has been ill, and there was some confusion with the real sub — we're still not sure what happened.

Frank Sr. and Paula seem a bit confused.

PRINCIPAL EVANS
Your son held a teacher-parent conference yesterday. He was plan-ning a class field trip to a French bread factory in Trenton. Do you see the problem we have?

PAULA
This is our fault, Principal Evans. Frank had been at Westbourne since he was a little boy. We had to take him out for personal rea-sons, away from his friends — you know how kids are. He's all alone here.

FRANK SR.
He's not alone. He has us.

INT. - ADMINISTRATOR'S OFFICE. - SAME TIME
Frank is sitting outside the Principal's office wearing his coat and tie, waiting for his parents to come out. Through the door, he can hear his father arguing with the Principal. Frank watches as JOANNA, the pretty cheerleader he saw earlier, walks up to a SCHOOL ADMINIS-TRATOR holding a note.

JOANNA
Ms. Davenport, I have a note to miss fifth and sixth period today. Doctor's appointment.

MS. DAVENPORT
One moment, Joanna.

As Ms. Davenport goes to answer the phone, Frank stares at Joanna, who nervously holds the note in her hands. She glances at Frank, then quickly looks away.

FRANK
You should fold it.

JOANNA
What?

FRANK
That note. It's a fake, right? You should fold it.

JOANNA
It's a note from my Mom. I have a doctor's...

FRANK
There's no crease in the paper. When your Mom hands you a note to miss school, the first thing you do is put it in your jacket pocket. A note like that is like gold — you wouldn't want to lose it. And if that note was in your jacket pocket — if it's real — where's the crease?

Joanna stares at Frank, then quickly grabs her note and folds it in quarters.

INT. - PRINCIPAL'S OFFICE. - DAY
Frank Sr. is trying to stay calm as he stares at Principal Evans.

PRINCIPAL EVANS
Sir, I have no choice but to suspend Frank for one week, and transfer him out of French and into German.

FRANK SR.
You're not suspending anyone. If you go after my son I'll go before the school board and ask them who's minding the store at Bellarmine Jefferson High. I'll ask my good friend Tom Walsh how it's possible for a little kid to teach a French class for an entire week without the Principal of the school knowing about it. I might even mention the fact that my son doesn't speak French.

INT. - FRANK'S APARTMENT. - DAY
Frank walks in from school, throws his books on a chair and opens the refrigerator. The radio is on and there's a bottle of wine on the counter next to some mail. Frank picks up a letter addressed to him.

FRANK
Mom, I'm home. Remember that girl Joanna I told you about?

Nobody answers, and Frank slowly walks toward the back bedroom door, which is closed. He opens the letter and pulls out his DRIVER'S LICENSE, smiling as he holds it up. He calls to his mother again.

FRANK
I asked her out today. I'm gonna take her to the Junior Prom. Mom?

Frank's about to knock when the bedroom door suddenly opens, and Paula walks out with JACK BARNES — the Rotary Club President — who wears a tailored black suit. Paula wears a dress and holds a tray of food.

PAULA
That's all there is, two bedrooms, but we're getting used to it. Frankie, you remember Dad's friend Jack Barnes from the club, he came by looking for your father — I was giving him a tour of the apartment.

JACK BARNES
Very spacious, Paula.

FRANK
Dad's at the store.

Frank stares at Jack, who walks over and picks up his HAT off the chair.

JACK BARNES
You look more like your old man every day. Thanks for the sandwich, Paula. I'll see ya later.

FRANK
Wait.

Frank walks to the couch, picks up a small ROTARY PIN that is lying on the cushions. He holds it up to Jack.

JACK BARNES
Thank you, Frank. That's the President's pin. I'd be in big trouble if I lost that.

Jack clips the pin to his jacket, turns, and walks out the door.

PAULA
Are you hungry, Frankie? I'll make you a sandwich.

Paula walks into the kitchen, opens the refrigerator, and starts making a sandwich.

PAULA
Jack wanted to talk business with your father. He thinks we should get a lawyer and sue the government, that it's not legal what they're doing to us.

Frank stares at his mother, who continues to make his sandwich. She walks over to him, her hands shaking as she hands him the plate.

PAULA
I'm going out for a few hours, visit some old friends from the tennis club. And when I get home we'll all have dinner together, right? But you won't say anything, because it's just silly, isn't it? How could we sue anybody?

Paula lights a cigarette, walks toward the door.

The Sets

This movie has about three times as many sets as any movie in its right mind should ever have. I thought *L.A. Confidential* was difficult because I counted 93 sets and we shot them in 40 or 50 places. When I broke down the first version of *Catch Me If You Can*, I counted 186 different sets and after that I couldn't count any more.

We started scouting in early October. I believe the location manager started a week or two before I did. We looked for five months, every day, almost all day long. I couldn't let myself think about how big the job was. The best advice I could give myself was just take it set by set. Put one foot down, look around, and then go take the next step.

We worked very hard to fool people into thinking they've just stepped off a bus into another era. The best thing anyone ever said to me about *L.A. Confidential* came from a friend of mine who took his 80-year-old father to the movie. Afterwards, his father told him that he had a great time watching it. He said, "Dad, did you know that was set back in the 1950s?" And he said, "It was? I didn't notice." To me that meant we had done it right. I hope someone comes to me after this film opens and says the same thing.

—JEANNINE OPPEWALL,
PRODUCTION DESIGNER

RIGHT: *The stationery store in Westchester, New York, owned by Frank's father in the movie, was actually shot in a shop in San Pedro, California.*

PAULA
Do you need some money, Frankie, a few dollars to buy some record albums? Here, take five dollars.

Paula holds out five dollars, and Frank walks toward her, reaches up, and takes the cigarette out of her mouth.

FRANK
You promised you were going to quit.

EXT. - ABAGNALE STATIONERS. - NEW ROCHELLE. - DAY
A large stationery store sits right in the middle of the upscale neighborhood of New Rochelle.

INT. - STATIONERY STORE. - DAY
Frank is working behind the counter of his father's store, gently placing a SILVER PEN across a velvet display pad. A WOMAN stares down at the pen.

FRANK
This is a .925 sterling silver Waldmann ballpoint pen with a two-color twist action top. Just turn it like this — the ink changes from black to blue. Nine dollars.

WOMAN
They have them in the city for six.

As the woman walks out of the store, Frank Sr. comes running out of his office, which doubles as the stockroom. He holds a letter in his hand.

FRANK SR.
I did it, Frank. The sons of bitches are running for the hills — read it and weep. I'm about to beat the United States government, take a look at that.

Frank Sr. hands Frank a letter.

FRANK SR.
See what it says — the I.R.S is backing off. They're gonna take their money and run...

FRANK
(*reading the letter*)
"No charges will be filed if two additional penalties are paid with interest dating back to March of 1961" —

FRANK SR.
They thought they could close me down, take our store, and I sent Uncle Sam running for the hills.

FRANK
How much are the penalties?

FRANK SR.
Don't worry, I'll negotiate a deal. I have it in writing now — they're on the ropes, black and white and cheap stock paper at that! We're gonna move back to New Rochelle, Frank, get a new house, a new car —

FRANK
A red Cadillac with white interior.

FRANK SR.
It's gonna take a little time, but we're gonna get it all back — every fur coat, every goddamn piece of silver! Come on, help me lock up. We're going to celebrate!

INT. - BAR. - EASTCHESTER. - DAY
Frank follows his father into the BAR, a neighborhood dive that is full of railway workers coming off the night shift. Frank and his father are greeted with cold stares from a handful of REGULARS who are drinking and watching a mounted black and white TV.

NEWSCASTER (V.O. ON TV)
The Warren Commission has concluded their investigation into the assassination of President Kennedy, and has found that Lee Harvey Oswald acted alone, with no evidence of conspiracy, domestic or foreign.

FRANK SR.
(*to the bartender*)
Bring us a couple of beers and two shots of Canadian.

BARTENDER
I need to see the kid's I.D.

FRANK SR.
This kid is the head salesman in my company. He's twenty-two and he's making five bills a week, so just bring the drinks and mind your business.

Frank and his father sit at a small table in the middle of the bar. Frank looks uncomfortable as his father lights a cigar.

FRANK
Maybe I should wait in the car.

FRANK SR.
Are you afraid of these men? Look at the way they sit, the way they dress, the way they drink. What are they, railway men? Cargo loaders? Those men haven't earned the right to judge us. What have they ever done?

The WAITRESS brings over the drinks, and Frank Sr. quickly downs both shots. He takes a DIME out of his pocket and sets it on the table.

FRANK SR.
Frank, I want you to take that dime and go put it in the jukebox. Pick something loud. We're celebrating.

Frank glances to the bar, where the MEN are quietly watching the TV. The JUKEBOX is directly under the television.

FRANK SR.
You know who I like? Lesley Gore.

FRANK
Dad...they're watching TV.

FRANK SR.
Yes. But in a moment they'll be listening to Lesley Gore. We're gonna teach the drunks to mind their manners.

FRANK
I think they know I'm not eighteen.

FRANK SR.
That's the blessing of looking older than you are — you get in the door.

FRANK
But I'm pretty sure they think...

FRANK SR.
No. People only know what you tell them.

Frank Sr. picks up the dime and holds it up to his son.

FRANK SR.
Take the dime, son. Just take the dime and walk over there like you

just closed a big deal. Walk over there like you got a roll of twenties right next to your pecker.

Frank gets out of his chair and nervously faces his Father.

FRANK SR.
And don't forget to smile while you're shoving it down their throats.

Frank holds his father's dime as he slowly walks toward the JUKEBOX. THE MEN AT THE BAR see him coming, slowly turn on their stools.

MAN #1
Don't play that thing.

BARTENDER
We're watching the news.

Frank nervously stands at the jukebox. Some of the men have gotten off their stools with drinks in hand.

MAN #1
We asked you not to do that, kid. The President is about to make a speech.

Frank looks toward his father, who sits back in his chair, smoking and smiling. Frank's hand shakes as he reaches out, drops the dime into the jukebox.

MAN #1
We're not gonna tell you again. Step away from the jukebox.

FRANK SR.
Why you bothering the kid? You got a problem, come bother me.

Frank watches as TWO DRUNKS walk toward his father. They both hold PITCHERS OF BEER in their hands.

FRANK SR.
Hit the button, Frank. You hit that goddamn button!

As Frank reaches out and hits the button, the men start to pour their beers over his father's head. Frank Sr. does nothing to stop them, the smile never leaving his face as he screams at his son.

> **FRANK SR.**
> That's right, Frank! Who are they! Who are they!

THE JUKEBOX springs to life, and WE HEAR LESLEY GORE singing "IT'S MY PARTY." The men continue to pour their beers over Frank Sr.'s head, the entire bar screaming with laughter.

> **FRANK SR.**
> Bus drivers! Security guards! Fry cooks! Now they understand! They can't win, Frank, they can't beat me!

EXT. - FRANK'S APARTMENT. - DAY
Frank steps off the bus from school, the bus pulls away and he walks toward home. He stops when he sees a BLACK LINCOLN TOWN CAR parked in front of his apartment.

INT. - FRANK'S APARTMENT. - DAY
Frank walks up the back stairs and enters through the kitchen door. He walks into the apartment, sees a BLACK SUIT JACKET hanging on the back of a chair, a pot of coffee brewing on the stove.

He walks toward the jacket and looks at the front lapel — searching for the President's pin. He is startled by a MAN who walks into the kitchen holding a coffee cup. The man's shirt sleeves are rolled up, and as he crosses to the stove he keeps his eyes on Frank.

> **FRANK**
> Stay away from her. I'm warning you, if you ever come back here...

The man pours himself a cup of coffee. He turns to Frank and motions to the living room.

> **MR. KESNER**
> Frank, I'm Dick Kesner. Put your books on the table. They're waiting for you.

INT. - APARTMENT LIVING ROOM. - DAY
AN OLD WOMAN dressed in a blue church dress is standing over a large box, CAREFULLY WRAPPING DISHES IN NEWSPAPER. There are several boxes already packed — and two giant glass cabinets have been picked clean.

Frank Sr. is sitting at the living room table drinking a cup of coffee as he reads a long legal document. His back is to the kitchen, his shoulders down.

Paula sits directly in front of her son, who has been placed in a chair at the head of the big table. Paula leans in, kisses Frank on the forehead.

> **PAULA**
> You don't have to be scared. I'm right here, Frank, I'll always be here. But there are laws — everything in this country has to be legal — so what we need to do is make some decisions. That's what Mr. Kesner is here for.

Mr. Kesner steps toward a very confused Frank.

> **MR. KESNER**
> Many times these decisions are left up to the courts. But that can be very expensive, Frank, people fighting over their children —

> **PAULA**
> Nobody is fighting. Just let me talk to my son. Look at me, Frank, nobody is fighting.

> **MR. KESNER**
> Your parents are just being smart. Why spend all of our money to

let someone else — a stranger who isn't even part of the family — why should we pay some judge to make that decision?

The OLD WOMAN stops packing and holds up two candlesticks. She speaks to Paula in French, and Paula snaps back at her. Paula smiles as she turns back to Frank.

> **PAULA**
> Frank, this is your grandmother. Her name is Eve Lavalier. She arrived this morning.

The OLD WOMAN smiles at Frank, and he gives her a small wave.

> **PAULA**
> Frank, you understand what we are saying to you? Your father and I are getting a divorce.

> **FRANK SR.**
> Nothing is going to change — we're all gonna see each other...

> **PAULA**
> Stop it. Please, Frank, don't —

Mr. Kesner hands Frank the DOCUMENT.

> **MR. KESNER**
> You don't have to read all this. Most of it is for your parents — boring adult business. But this paragraph here, this is important. Because it states who you are going to live with after the divorce. Who's custody you will be in.

> **PAULA**
> And there's a blank space right here, you see that?

Frank stares at the blank line, slowly nods.

> **MR. KESNER**
> Now I want you to go into the kitchen, sit at the table and write down the name. You can take as long as you want — but when you come back in here, I want there to be a name written on that line.

> **FRANK SR.**
> Frank, just write down a name and this will all be over.

> **FRANK**
> A name?

> **MR. KESNER**
> Your mother or your father. Just put the name there, it's as simple as that. And don't look so scared, this isn't a test.

Mr. Kesner hands Frank the pen. He looks at his mother and father.

> **MR. KESNER**
> There is no wrong answer.

I **was** raised about twenty-five miles north of New York City, in Westchester County, New York. I was one of four children, the so-called middle child of the family. I went to a private Catholic school.

One day, when I was in the tenth grade, I was taken out of class and driven to this stone building that said Family Court. I didn't understand what that meant. When I arrived, court was already in session, so I was ushered into the back of the courtroom. My parents were standing before the judge. The judge saw me at the back of the room and motioned for me to approach the bench. I walked up and stood between my parents.

The judge said that my parents were getting a divorce and I had to tell the court which parent I wanted to live with, my mother or my father. I remember that the judge never looked at me.

I got very upset and started to cry. I was sixteen years old. I needed my mother and my father. I loved both of them. Here a complete stranger was telling me to choose one of them, and there was no way I could do that without hurting one of them. It was a lot easier for me to turn and run out of the courtroom, which is what I did.

The judge called for a ten-minute recess. By the time my parents got outside, I was gone.

My mother didn't see me again for seven years. My father, unfortunately, never saw me again.

—Frank W. Abagnale, on the movie

41

EXT. - EASTCHESTER. - DAY
Frank is running through town — the pen clutched in his hand — his school bag flying off his shoulder —

INT. - FRANK'S APARTMENT. - FLASHBACK
Frank holds the pen in his hand. He stares at his mother and father for a BEAT, then looks at the OLD WOMAN. She says something to him in French, then walks over and hands him a small MODEL AIRPLANE with a bow tied around the tail.

> **PAULA**
> What do you say, Frank?

INT. - EASTCHESTER TRAIN STATION. - DUSK
Frank runs up to the ticket window at the TRAIN STATION.

> **FRANK**
> One ticket to Grand Central, please.

> **TICKET CLERK**
> Three dollars and fifty cents.

> **FRANK**
> Can I write you a check?

INT. - PERPIGNAN PRISON. - FRANCE. - DAY
THE CELL DOOR IS PULLED OPEN, and Frank slowly walks out and faces Carl Hanratty, who is holding a pair of HANDCUFFS. Hanratty gets a glimpse inside the cell — and quickly turns away.

> **HANRATTY**
> Come on, Frank. It's time to go.

Carl puts the handcuffs on Frank, who can barely stay on his feet as he slowly turns to Warden Garren.

> **FRANK**
> Your wife is sleeping with one of the weekend guards. Just thought you should know.

INT. - HOTEL ROOM. - FRANCE. - NIGHT
Carl Hanratty, Amdursky, and Fox are all watching Frank as he sits naked in a bathtub, his handcuffs still on as he tries to shave his beard.

INT. - HOTEL ROOM. - FRANCE. - NIGHT
Frank has one hand HANDCUFFED to a chair, and both legs SHACKLED to the corner of the bed. He's eating a sandwich and drinking a glass of milk as Hanratty sits across from him.

> **FRANK**
> I want to call my father.

> **HANRATTY**
> You can call him when we get to New York. We leave for the airport in seven hours. Just sit there and be quiet.

Frank looks around the room.

> **FRANK**
> On the other side of the hotel they have suites that face the park.

> **HANRATTY**
> This is the only room the FBI could afford.

> **FRANK**
> It's okay, Carl. I've stayed in worse.

LEFT INSET: The crew truck that Steven Spielberg used to capture Leonardo DiCaprio running through the streets.

INT. - TIMES SQUARE HOTEL. - NIGHT
Frank wears blue pajamas as he's THROWN OUT OF A DILAPIDATED TIMES SQUARE HOTEL ROOM BY THE NIGHT MANAGER, who is dragging him toward the door.

The Eraser

It's always hard to describe what it is about a place that speaks to a designer. The place has to have a special kind of poetry all its own, it has to say something to you. You walk into a place and you can imagine the scenes that are required for the story unfolding in front of you. Los Angeles is good that way; it offers an incredibly varied diet of architecture and plant life.

I always say the pencil has two ends. It has the lead end and the eraser end. When you make a period movie, you use more of the eraser than you do of the lead. It's more expensive to take out than it is to put in. So, we spend an enormous amount of time finding creative ways to disguise what doesn't work — hiding it behind bushes, hiding it with boxes, and painting it away. Slowly, you peel back the layers until you feel you're where you're supposed to be.

—JEANNINE OPPEWALL, PRODUCTION DESIGNER

SUPER: AUGUST, 1964

> **MANAGER**
> I don't want to hear your story. That's two checks that bounced. Do you know how much trouble I'm in?

> **FRANK**
> The bank made a mistake, Mr. Mudrick. I'll write you a check right now! Please, it's midnight, I have no place to go.

The Manager pushes Frank into the cage elevator.

> **MANAGER**
> You're a goddamn kid. Go home.

INT. - TIMES SQUARE HOTEL ROOM. - NIGHT
A decrepit Times Square hotel room. Bars on the windows, sirens approaching from all directions. Frank lies back on a small bed staring up at his NEW YORK DRIVER'S LICENSE — which is a simple I.D. CARD with no pictures. Frank uses a pen to make a COPY of the license, changing the date of birth from 1948 to 1938 — and the name ABAGNALE to TAYLOR.

Frank turns out the lamp, stares up at the ceiling — nervously watches as the shadows dance over his head.

His eyes never close.

INT. - MANHATTAN SAVINGS AND TRUST. - DAY
Frank holds a BLACK BRIEFCASE as he stands in front of a FEMALE BANK TELLER holding a CHASE MANHATTAN CHECK.

Icarus

The part captures what it's like for a young man who doesn't have the right guidance in his life. He is let out on his own and is like Icarus. He goes to the utmost extreme, he makes up his own rules as he goes along. The fact that it's a story about crime is irrelevant to me. It's about human will power and the fact this kid was able to con the world for several years from the age of sixteen on. It's about human potential.

—LEONARDO DiCAPRIO

FRANK
My boss sent me to Brooklyn, then Queens, now he wants me in
Long Island to take a few clients out for a night on the town....

ASHLEY
I'm sorry, but we're not allowed to cash checks from other banks.
How would we know if they were any good?

FRANK
What's your name?

ASHLEY
Ashley.

FRANK
Ashley, do you know what I found on the sidewalk out there?

ABOVE: *Steven Spielberg with producers Laurie MacDonald and Walter Parkes on location during the shooting of* Catch Me If You Can.

On the Run

*C*atch Me If You Can reads like a simple two-character story, but in the end, proved to be a very complicated production. Aside from two longish scenes between Frank and his father, almost every other scene is less than a page and calls for a different location, time, and costume change. Most days we shot a half-day in one location and then moved to another location. In a way, the shoot imitated the story. We were constantly on the run.

Catch Me was difficult in a different way than *Gladiator* or *Minority Report*. We weren't shooting in space or Ancient Rome, so our work was not in service to the special effects. We had a straightforward story but on a day-to-day level, we were constantly dealing with difficult production issues. It was actually liberating to work within a smaller budget. We were forced to solve problems creatively instead of throwing money at them. We tried to make a big Hollywood movie with a sense of economy and discipline, and hopefully, all that energy comes out on screen.

—WALTER F. PARKES AND
LAURIE MACDONALD, PRODUCERS

Frank reaches down to his small BRIEFCASE, struggles to get it open. He reaches inside and pulls out a SMALL SILVER PENDANT.

> **FRANK**
> I'll bet this slipped right off....

As Frank stands up, the BANK MANAGER is standing in front of Ashley. He looks at Frank, then at the pendant.

> **BANK MANAGER**
> Is there something I can help you with, son?

SMASH CUT

ANOTHER BANK —
Frank, now wearing a shirt and tie, stands in front of an OLD FEMALE TELLER.

> **FRANK**
> I just need to buy a birthday present for my grandmother.

SMASH CUT

ANOTHER TELLER — FRANK LOOKS LIKE A COLLEGE STUDENT —

> **FRANK**
> The midterm is next week and my books were stolen....

SMASH CUT

FRANK looks tired, his clothes wrinkled as he slides a CHASE MANHATTAN check over to a young FEMALE TELLER.

> **FRANK**
> It's just five dollars. Nobody would have to know.

FEMALE TELLER
I'm sorry. But we're not allowed to take checks from people we
don't know.

EXT. - BANK. - DAY
As Frank walks out of the bank, he watches A PILOT AND TWO
FLIGHT ATTENDANTS step out of a cab right in front of him.
They are all laughing as they head for the revolving doors of the
VAN WYCK HOTEL.

Frank watches as the PILOT SLIPS THE
DOORMAN A FIVE DOLLAR BILL.

INT. - VAN WYCK HOTEL. - DAY
Frank follows the Pilot into the lobby of
the Van Wyck, sees the hotel MANAGER
rushing over to greet him.

The entire lobby seems to be focused on
the Pilot, with BELLMEN running over to
carry his bags — the FLIGHT ATTEN-
DANTS following his every move.

PILOT
(*southern accent*)
What do you think, Angelo? The toma-
toes are ripe this afternoon

Frank turns to an aging BELLMAN.

FRANK
Excuse me, is that a famous pilot?

I **found** working New York
very challenging.
The logistics of filming in Manhattan
are almost beyond my comprehension.
We were able to block off six city
blocks and bring in period cars,
wardrobe, and people. It was very
interesting to see Park Avenue transformed from present day into Park
Avenue of 1964.

The challenge also came from
eliminating modern elements within
each frame. It's difficult because
Manhattan is in a constant state of
flux. Things are being torn out, new
buildings are going up, and the feel of
1964 almost doesn't exist today in New
York even with the classical buildings.

—Janusz Kaminski,
Director of Photography

BELLMAN
No. He's just one of those airline jerks. Just because you fly at thirty thousand feet, doesn't make you God.

Frank watches as the Pilot walks into the elevator, the Flight Attendants by his side. As the elevator doors close, the pilot is WHISTLING the theme to "High and Mighty."

INT. - ABAGNALE STATIONERY STORE. - DAY
Frank Sr. stands alone in his store reading a POSTCARD.

FRANK (V.O.)
Dear Dad...I've decided to become an airline pilot. I've applied at all the big airlines, and have several promising interviews lined up.

EXT. - PAY PHONE. - NEW YORK. - DAY
A packed street corner in the center of New York. Frank is eating a hot dog as he talks on a PAY PHONE.

PAN AM OPERATOR (V.O.)
Pan Am, how may I help you?

FRANK
(*southern accent*)
I'd like to speak to someone about a uniform.

PAN AM OPERATOR
Hold for purchasing.

Frank turns and looks directly behind him, where WE SEE the FIFTY STORIES OF THE PAN AM BUILDING standing tall in the middle of the city.

PURCHASING SUPERVISOR (V.O.)
Purchasing.

FRANK
Yes. I'm a co-pilot based out of San Francisco. I flew a flight into New York last night, and I'm leaving for Paris in three hours.

PURCHASING SUPERVISOR (V.O.)
How can we help you?

FRANK
I sent my uniform out to be cleaned through the hotel...

PURCHASING SUPERVISOR (V.O.)
Let me guess. They lost the uniform. Happens all the time.

EXT. - NEW YORK STREET. - DAY
As the telephone conversation continues, WE SEE Frank running down a busy street, a big smile on his face as he cuts in and out of an endless stream of people.

PURCHASING SUPERVISOR (V.O.)
Go down to the Well-Built Uniform Company at Ninth and Broadway — they're our uniform supplier. I'll tell Mister Rosen you're coming.

INT. - WELL-BUILT UNIFORM COMPANY. - DAY
Frank poses in front of a full-length mirror wearing a brand new PAN AM UNIFORM. MISTER ROSEN kneels in front of him, cuffing his pants. In the B.G., WE SEE rows and rows of uniforms waiting to be shipped.

ROSEN
What's your rank?

FRANK
I'm a co-pilot.

ROSEN
Right seat. I figured as much. You look too young to be a pilot.

FRANK
I just turned 27.

Mr. Rosen places THREE GOLD STRIPES on both arms of Frank's jacket. He looks up at Frank, sees that he's sweating.

ROSEN
Why so nervous?

FRANK
How would you feel if you lost your uniform first week on the job?

ROSEN
Relax — Pan Am's got lots of uniforms. It's gonna be $164.

FRANK
I'll write you a check.

ROSEN
Sorry. No checks, no cash. You have to fill out your employee I.D. number, then I'll bill Pan Am and they'll take it out of your next pay check.

Frank thinks about this, starts to smile.

FRANK
Even better.

EXT. - NEW YORK. - DAY
Frank is whistling the theme to "High and Mighty" as he walks down Broadway in his new uniform, enjoying the obvious glances he is getting from men and women who pass by. He sees a little boy pointing at him, and he gives the boy a playful salute.

LITTLE BOY
Are you a real live pilot?

Frank can't help but smile as he drops his briefcase in the nearest trash can.

INT. - MANHATTAN SAVINGS AND TRUST. - DAY
A FEMALE BANK TELLER is sneaking glances at Frank as she counts out his money on the counter. The BANK MANAGER is standing next to the teller, offering him a tray of cookies and a cup of coffee. He takes both.

BANK TELLER
That's eighty, ninety, one hundred dollars. You have yourself a great time in Paris.

FRANK
I always do.

INT. - TIMES SQUARE HOTEL ROOM. - NIGHT
Frank's shoes are freshly polished and sitting on the floor of the dilapidated hotel room. Frank is standing at the mirror putting Brylcream in his hair, staring at himself as the PILOT'S UNIFORM lies alone on the bed behind him.

He drops a new stack of CHASE MANHATTAN checks on the bed — the name on the top reads: FRANK TAYLOR.

INT. - VAN WYCK HOTEL LOBBY. - NEW YORK - DAY
Frank stands in uniform at the front desk.

FRONT DESK CLERK
Have you stayed with us before?

FRANK
No, I've been based on the West Coast. Okay if I write you a check for the room?

FRONT DESK CLERK
No problem, Sir.

FRANK
I was also wondering if you could cash a personal check for me. I've got a date with a cute little hostess this evening.

Frank pulls out his Chase Manhattan check book.

FRONT DESK CLERK
For airline personnel we cash personal checks up to one hundred dollars. For payroll checks we will cash up to three hundred dollars.

FRANK
Three hundred for a payroll check?

FRONT DESK CLERK
That's right. Do you have one?

Frank stares at the clerk for a long BEAT.

FRANK
Do you know where I could buy a typewriter?

INT. - VAN WYCK HOTEL SUITE. - NIGHT
CLOSE ON: A BLANK COUNTER CHECK

The ELECTRIC STRIKING BALL of an IBM ELECTRIC TYPEWRITER is going over the same words again and again, making them appear PRINTED.

FRANK (V.O.)
Dear Dad. I have been accepted to Pan Am's flight school, and will be starting my training immediately. How are you? Please

The props in *Catch Me if You Can* were particularly important in telling the story. There's a scene where Leo goes into a store and buys all these Pan Am model planes. You don't know why he's buying them until the camera cuts to a bathtub full of planes. He is soaking off the labels. That's a good example of how important the props can be in telling the story.

Gathering together the props is always like a big scavenger hunt. I am always at antique malls, swap meets, thrift stores, estate sales, and on eBay. When I got this job, I was in Detroit on another movie and I was able to shop out there. It was an uptapped area and I probably got 60% of the movie there — luggage, strollers, bikes, you name it. Then I found 20 Pan Am bags at an Aviation show in Long Beach and bought some others on eBay. It's very challenging to pull together a period movie.

—Steve Melton, Propmaster

get in touch with Joanna Carlson at Bellarmine Jefferson High School, and let her know that I am sorry I couldn't take her to the Junior Prom.

The top of the phony check reads: PAN AMERICAN WORLD AIR-WAYS EMPLOYEE NUMBER 15415. PAY TO THE ORDER OF FRANK TAYLOR $299.12

INT. - HOTEL BATHROOM. - MORNING
Frank kneels over the bathtub, looking down at the PLASTIC 707 MODEL AIRPLANE that his grandmother gave to him. The small plane is soaking in the tub, floating upside down in a pool of bubbles.

CLOSE ON: THE WING OF THE MODEL PLANE.

The PAN AM LOGO is on the tail. WE WATCH as a TWEEZER lifts the corner of the logo right off the plastic, carefully slipping it off the wing so that the words PAN AMERICAN WORLD AIRWAYS hang in mid-air.

ON FRANK: meticulously placing the LOGO on top of the check he has just made. The words stick to the paper, and he quickly takes the check and places it in the middle of a hotel BIBLE. He sticks the Bible under his bed, the way a kid breaks in a new baseball glove.

INT. - CHASE MANHATTAN BANK. - DAY
Frank is still in uniform as he walks past two MALE TELLERS and deliberately approaches a YOUNG FEMALE TELLER.

> **FRANK**
> I was wondering if you could cash this payroll check for me.

Frank takes the check out of a phony PAN AM ENVELOPE and hands it to the TELLER. The PAN AM LOGO on the check is crooked and off center, the type blurred and almost illegible.

> **FRANK**
> You have beautiful eyes.

The TELLER smiles at Frank, barely glances at the check as she opens her CASH DRAWER.

> **TELLER**
> How would you like it?

INT. - CARNEGIE HOBBY SHOP. - DAY
A small HOBBY SHOP in Times Square. Frank sets 15 BOXES of PAN AM MODEL AIRPLANES on the counter in front of the owner.

> **HOBBY SHOP OWNER**
> That's a lot of planes.

> **FRANK**
> I give them away at Christmas to needy children.

> **HOBBY SHOP OWNER**
> Will this be cash or check?

Frank watches as the OWNER starts to ring them up on a cash register that is exactly like the one in his father's store.

> **FRANK**
> Cash.

The Viewer's Eyes

In the U.S., my official title is Director of Photography; in Europe, it's called cinematographer. I direct the photography and the visual language of the film. I am responsible for telling the story through light or through lack of light. I create the shadows. To a certain degree, I'm the viewer's eyes. I let the viewers see what they're supposed to see simply by either putting the light on the actors or taking the light away. It's primarily an artistic profession and form of expression but it also requires extensive technical knowledge of lighting equipment, cameras, lenses, dollies, and cranes.

—JANUSZ KAMINSKI, DIRECTOR OF PHOTOGRAPHY

INT. - VAN WYCK HOTEL SUITE. - NIGHT
An episode of THE RIFLEMAN is on the black and white TV in the massive hotel room. A ROOM SERVICE CART sits next to the bed, piled high with half-eaten plates of french fries, hamburgers, and slices of apple pie. The bottles of ketchup and mustard and Coca-Cola have all had their labels picked clean.

CLOSE ON: A HOTEL BATHTUB FILLED WITH MODEL AIRPLANES THAT ARE SOAKING IN WARM WATER.

Frank sits at a desk, pulls a CHECK from the carriage of an electric typewriter. The check is perfectly centered, the Pan Am logo straight, the lines and words looking thick and heavy — as if they were printed.

Frank takes the check and sets it on the hotel bed, where 100 FRESHLY MADE CHECKS are sitting in neatly stacked piles.

INT. - VAN WYCK HOTEL LOBBY. - MORNING
Frank walks downstairs in his uniform, CHECK IN HAND. The HOTEL MANAGER rushes over to greet him.

> **MANAGER**
> What can I do for you, Mr. Taylor?
>
> **FRANK**
> I need a little spending money, Charles.
>
> **MANAGER**
> I'm sorry, Sir, we won't have any cash until the banks open in a hour. But I'm sure they can cash your check at the airport.
>
> **FRANK**
> The airport? Who cashes checks at the airport?
>
> **MANAGER**
> The airlines, Sir. They've always taken care of their own.

INT. - LA GUARDIA AIRPORT. - MORNING
Frank is standing with several AIRLINE EMPLOYEES waiting to cash a check at one of the ticket counters. He looks at a TWA PILOT who is standing next to

An airline official who made a statement to the police concerning my escapades offered what seemed to him a logical explanation: "You simply don't expect a man in a pilot's uniform, with proper credentials and obvious knowledge of jump procedures, to be an impostor, dammit!"

—Frank W. Abagnale, from his book

him, sees the way the pilot has rolled up his sleeves, tied his tie. He stares at the Pilot's I.D. BADGE, which is a laminated picture clipped to the front of his jackets.

TWA PILOT
You have a good day, Frances. I'll bring pictures of the twins next week.

Pilot takes his cash, turns back toward Frank.

FRANK
Morning.

The PILOT turns and looks at Frank.

TWA PILOT
Morning. What's Pan Am doing out here at La Guardia? Pan Am doesn't fly into La Guardia.

Frank stares at the Pilot, has no idea what to say.

TWA PILOT
You working charters?

FRANK
Yeah. Charters.

TWA PILOT
I figured as much. What kind of equipment you on?

FRANK
(*no idea*)
General Electric.

TWA PILOT
General Electric? What the hell do you fly, washing machines?

INT. - LA GUARDIA. - DAY
Frank is running out of the airport.

INT. - PAN AM BUILDING. - DAY
The massive CORPORATE OFFICES of PAN AM, which look out over Manhattan. Frank, dressed like a student and holding a notebook, gets out of the elevator and walks up to a RECEPTIONIST who sits in front of a door marked: PAUL MORGAN, DIRECTOR OF AIRLINE SECURITY.

FRANK
I'm Frank Black from Monroe High School. I have an appointment with Mister Morgan.

RECEPTIONIST
You're the young man writing the article for the school paper?

FRANK
Yes, Ma'am. I want to know everything there is to know about being a pilot.

INT. - PAN AM BUILDING. - DAY
PAUL MORGAN, 70s, a small rock of a man, walks with Frank through a large GALLERY which shows the history of PAN AM in black and white pictures and detailed PLASTIC MODELS. Frank has a CAMERA around his neck, and every so often he snaps a picture of Morgan.

MORGAN
What's your name, son?

FRANK
Frank.

MORGAN
So you want to know about the exciting life of a real live pilot?

Well today's your lucky day, Frank, because I was one of the best. And I'd still be — if they hadn't grounded me.

Morgan turns to Frank and shows him his left eye.

MORGAN
Detached retina. It's like staring into the sun all day long.

FRANK
Which airports does Pan Am fly to? How much do pilots make a year? Who tells them where they're gonna fly to?

MORGAN
Hold it. Slow down. One at a time?

FRANK
What does it mean when one pilot says to another pilot, "What kind of equipment are you on?"

MORGAN
He's asking what kind of plane he flies. DC-8. 707.

FRANK
Can you tell me about the I.D. badges I've seen pilots wear?

MORGAN
A pilot is required to carry two things with him at all times. His airline personnel badge, which is similar to this Pan Am badge I'm wearing, and his FAA license.

Morgan pulls an old FAA LICENSE out of his wallet.

FRANK
Do you think I could make a copy of this license to put in my article?

MORGAN
You can have it, Frank. It expired three years ago.

FRANK
What about your I.D. badge? Do you have an extra one I could borrow?

MORGAN
I'm afraid I can't help you there. These badges are special ordered from Polaroid. The only way to get one is to become a real live pilot for Pan American Airways.

INT. - POLAROID CORPORATE OFFICES. - NEW YORK. - DAY
A LARGE OFFICE IN NEW YORK CITY. A POLAROID SALESMAN has opened a SAMPLE BOOK and is showing off page after page of LAMINATED I.D. BADGES. FRANK wears a suit and tie as he sits across from the salesman examining the book.

FRANK
What's your name?

POLAROID SALESMAN
Timothy.

FRANK
Today's your lucky day, Harvey. Caribbean Air is going to expand our routes next year to include most of the East coast, which means we're gonna need several thousand new badges.

POLAROID SALESMAN
As you can see, we make the I.D. badges for almost every major airline.

Frank points to one of the badges.

FRANK
I like that one. Which airline is that?

POLAROID SALESMAN
That's Pan Am. Why don't you take the brochure on that one.

FRANK
Thanks. I'm sure we'll be in touch.

Frank heads for the door — stopping just as he enters the hall.

FRANK
I hate to bother you, but my boss wanted me to bring back an actual I.D. badge, not a brochure.

POLAROID SALESMAN
That's no problem, Mister Taylor. We make all the badges right here with this equipment.

The Salesman motions to a large CAMERA AND LAMINATOR.

POLAROID SALESMAN
I can make you one in a few seconds.

Frank sits in front of the camera.

FRANK
I have an idea. Why don't you use me as the subject?

INT - KENNEDY AIRPORT. - DAY
Frank's pockets are overflowing with cash, and he's got an envelope stuffed with checks in his hand. He's walking through KENNEDY AIRPORT, jacket over his shoulder, sleeves rolled up — his authentic PAN AM I.D. BADGE secured to the pocket of his shirt.

TWO YOUNG BOYS are smiling at him, and he walks over and hands them each a pair of PAN AM PILOT'S WINGS.

FRANK
Always do good in school.

He watches as FOUR PRETTY STEWARDESSES move through the terminal, the women moving like runway models as they cut through the passengers and walk past the TWA COUNTER and onto the plane. Frank moves toward the counter, his eyes never leaving the girls.

TWA TICKET AGENT
Are you dead-heading?

FRANK
What?

TWA TICKET AGENT
Are you my dead-head to Miami?

Frank stares at the woman for a long BEAT. He looks toward the plane, then turns back to the terminal — where the two little BOYS and their parents are waving at him.

FRANK
Yes. I'm your dead-head.

The AGENT holds out her hand, and Frank hands her his I.D. BADGE and Morgan's FAA license, which has been cropped at the top where Morgan's name used to be. She barely glances at either.

TWA TICKET AGENT
You're a little late, but the jump seat is open. Have a nice flight.

FRANK
Good. The jump seat is open.

Frank nervously looks toward the plane as the Ticket Agent hands him a PINK SLIP.

FRANK
Ya know, it's been awhile since I've done this — which is the jump seat again?

The Ticket Agent starts to laugh, and Frank laughs with her.

INT. - TWA 707. - DAY
MARCI, a cute 27-year-old TWA STEWARDESS with short blonde hair and glasses, stands at the front of the plane smiling at Frank — who holds out his pink boarding slip.

MARCI
Are you my dead-head?

INT. - COCKPIT. - 707. - DAY
Frank is led into the cockpit by Marci, trying not to react to the inten-

sity of the tiny space. He immediately looks around for the jump-seat — or any seat — but sees nothing.

MARCI
Frank, this is Captain Oliver. That's John Larkin, the Co-Pilot, this is Fred Tulley, flight engineer.

FRANK
Frank Taylor, Pan Am. Thanks for giving me a lift.

CAPTAIN OLIVER
Go ahead and take a seat, Frank, we're about to push. What kind of equipment you on?

FRANK
707.

CAPTAIN OLIVER
You turning around on the red eye?

FRANK
No. I'm jumping puddles for the next few months. Gotta earn my keep running leap frogs for the weak and weary.

CAPTAIN OLIVER
No shame in that. We all did it.

Frank continues to search for the JUMP SEAT, the panic starting to show on his face as Marci reaches her hand around to the back of the cockpit and pulls down the small METAL SEAT.

MARCI
There you go. Would you like a drink after take-off?

Frank quickly sits in the jump-seat, his hands shaking as he tries to strap himself in.

FRANK
A glass of milk, please.

EXT. - KENNEDY AIRPORT RUNWAY. - DAY
THE TWA JET is shooting down the runway at Kennedy airport.

CLOSE ON: FRANK — inside the cockpit — his hands gripping the sides of the JUMP-SEAT, his body and face clenched into a silent scream as the plane lifts off, banking left as it shoots out over the water.

FRANK (V.O.)
Dear Dad. Today was graduation.

Frank is staring out the cockpit window in disbelief, the way all kids do the first time they ride in a plane.

INT. - FRANK SR.'S EASTCHESTER APARTMENT. - DAY
Frank Sr. struggles as he walks into his apartment carrying a large box, which he sets on the floor next to his mail. As he stands up holding a LETTER, WE SEE that the apartment is now COVERED IN BOXES, and it resembles the stock room of his store.

FRANK (V.O.)
I am sending you a picture of me in my uniform, so that you can show it to mom, and let her know that I am a pilot for the greatest airline in the world.

INT. - TWA 707. - LATER IN FLIGHT
Frank walks through the COCKPIT DOOR, sees Marci preparing drinks at the beverage station.

MARCI
Hello, dead-head. Enjoying your free ride?

FRANK
Marci, did you drop this?

Frank takes a SMALL GOLD NECKLACE out of his jacket pocket.

FRANK
Must have slipped right off your neck.

INT. - FRANK'S HOTEL SUITE. - MIAMI. - NIGHT
The largest suite in the hotel. Room service carts are stacked by the door, overflowing with bottles of pop and champagne. In the bedroom Frank is lying on top of Marci — losing his virginity — not moving — just staring down at her with a bizarre look on his face. The lights are low, the radio is on.

FRANK
Are all hostesses as nice as you?

MARCI
Stewardess. You know we like to be called stewardess now. Why are you stopping?

FRANK
I want to tell you something, Marci. This is by far the best date I've ever been on.

INT. - HOTEL LOBBY. - DAY
An exhausted Frank is standing at the front desk staring down at his HOTEL BILL, a look of mild shock on his face as he reads the number at the bottom.

FRANK
Four hundred and eleven dollars?

INT. - MIAMI MUTUAL BANK. - DAY
Frank is wearing his pilot's uniform as he walks up to LUCY, the pretty ASSISTANT MANAGER of a large bank.

LUCY
Welcome to Miami Mutual Bank, how may I help you?

FRANK
My name is Frank Taylor, and I'm a co-pilot for Pan Am. I'd like to cash this check and then take you out for a steak dinner.

INT. - MIAMI HOTEL ROOM. - NIGHT
Frank is jumping on the bed with LUCY, who is laughing uncontrollably as their heads almost hit the ceiling.

LUCY
Okay, enough! We have to stop, I can't breathe! I'm getting dressed.

FRANK
A little more! We can break the bed!

LUCY
How old did you say you were? I have to get home and get some sleep.

FRANK
It's only midnight.

LUCY
One of my tellers got married last night, and I'm gonna be short-handed all week.

Frank stops jumping.

FRANK
What if I came and helped you out down at the bank?

LUCY
Now why would a Pan Am Pilot want to help work in my stupid bank?

About the Screenplay

The thing I loved most about Frank's story was that it reminded me of some of the films I grew up loving from the 1960s and 1970s. *Butch Cassidy and the Sundance Kid, The Sting, Cool Hand Luke, One Flew Over the Cuckoo's Nest* — great movies about outsiders who challenge the disposition of society. They were all criminals, yet you couldn't help but root for them because they were so clever and charming. I guess I had always wanted to write a script in the tone of those films, and Frank's story provided the perfect excuse to try.

I interviewed Frank many times before I started to write, and each time we would talk about his various cons, and then the conversation would inevitably switch over to a discussion of his father — whom he loved very much. This father-son relationship became the emotional center of the script, and it changed the structure of the movie from a simple cat-and-mouse thriller to a complex family drama.

Frank's search for his own identity, for the unconditional love of his parents, and for the childhood that his father promised to him are what drives the script forward. And with each step he takes away from home, away from his own innocence, he moves closer to the man who will ultimately catch him, and take his father's place — FBI Agent Carl Hanratty.

—JEFF NATHANSON, SCREENWRITER

Frank holds her close, dances her toward the bed —

> **FRANK**
> To be close to you.

INT. - MIAMI MUTUAL BANK. - DAY
Frank is standing with Lucy behind the counter of the bank, watching as she feeds a stack of CHECKS into a MICR ENCODING MACHINE.

> **LUCY**
> We feed the checks through the MICR machine, which uses special ink to encode the account numbers on the bottom of the checks.

> **FRANK**
> What numbers?

> **LUCY**
> See the numbers on the bottom of the checks. Those are called routing numbers.

> **FRANK**
> Where do the checks get routed to?

> **LUCY**
> Well, I'm not exactly sure. Nobody ever asked before.

INT. - NEW JERSEY AUCTION HOUSE. - DAY
A SIGN READS: FORECLOSURE AUCTION — NEW JERSEY CENTRAL BANK

WE SEE rows of desks, chairs, couches, and cash drawers — everything you could possibly find at a bank. The AUCTIONEER stands in front of a room filled with BANKERS and BUSINESSMEN in dark suits.

> **AUCTIONEER**
> Our next item up for bid is also from the Jersey Central Bank foreclosure. This is a MICR encoder, a machine used to encode bank checks. Do I have an opening bid?

In the audience, Frank, dressed in a suit, smiles as he raises his paddle.

EXT. - CHASE MANHATTAN BANK. - DAY
Frank wears his uniform as he pulls up to the front of the bank in a brand new RED CADILLAC. He parks in front of the fire hydrant, starts walking toward the door, which swings open for him.

INT. - NEW YORK RESTAURANT. - DAY
Frank Sr., his suit wrinkled, briefcase in hand, is led toward a center table in an upscale restaurant, which looks out onto Madison Avenue. Frank is waiting for him, a small wrapped present in front of him, a bottle of champagne chilling on ice. He stands up and hugs his father, the two men embracing for a long BEAT.

> **FRANK SR.**
> Jesus, look at you? My son the birdman. That is some uniform, Frank.

The WAITER walks over holding a silver tray. They each take a small FORK off the tray.

> **FRANK SR.**
> This fork is ice cold.

> **FRANK**
> It's a chilled salad fork. Open the present.

The two men sit across from each other, and Frank Sr. opens the gift. He pulls out a set of car keys.

> **FRANK**
> Look out that window.

Frank Sr. looks out the window, sees a brand new CADILLAC parked in front of the hotel.

FRANK
That's a 1965 Cadillac De Ville convertible with white interior, split seats, air conditioning —

Frank Sr. smiles, slowly puts the keys back in the box.

FRANK SR.
You're giving me a Cadillac?

FRANK
After lunch why don't you drive over and pick up Mom. It's her birthday next week, you'll knock her socks off.

FRANK SR.
She's beautiful. Only I'm gonna get myself another white one. I already ordered it. You keep that one, Frank, maybe one day we'll race to Atlantic City.

Frank Sr. slides the box over to Frank.

FRANK
If you want you could borrow the car for a few days — I could pick it up next week.

FRANK SR.
You worried about me? You think I can't buy my own car? Two mice fell in a bucket of cream, Frank. Which one am I?

FRANK
I went by the store today.

FRANK SR.
I had to close the store for a few days. It's all about timing, Frank, the goddamn government knows that. They hit you when you're down, and I wasn't gonna let them take it from me. So I just shut the doors myself, called their bluff.

The Hanratty character was based on a real FBI Agent who was tracking Frank, and who ultimately took him out of prison and let him work with the FBI. What I like about this character is that he is completely stuck in the rules and social conventions of his time, yet he has to catch someone who is shattering those rules with every step he takes.

In the end this was the point of the script, to mirror the simplicity of Frank's "crimes" with the simple world that was once the United States. And while Agent Hanratty is desperate to catch Frank, what he's really trying to catch is a world that no longer exists — a world that was built on trust and a firm handshake.

—Jeff Nathanson, Screenwriter

FRANK
Have you told Mom?

Frank Sr. leans in, starts to whisper.

FRANK SR.
She's so stubborn, your mother. But don't worry, I'm not gonna let her go without a fight. I've been fighting for her since the day we met.

FRANK
Of all those soldiers, you were the one who took her home.

FRANK SR.
Two hundred men were sitting in that little social hall watching her dance. Do you remember the name of that village?

FRANK
Montrichard.

FRANK SR.
I didn't speak a word of French, and six weeks later, she was my wife.

The WAITER brings over a bottle of champagne, pouring two glasses.

FRANK SR.
My son bought me a Cadillac today. I think that calls for a toast. To the best damn pilot in the sky.

FRANK
It's not what you think. I'm just a co-pilot.

FRANK SR.
You see these people staring at you, Frank? These are the most powerful people in New York City, and they keep peeking over their shoulders, wondering where you're going tonight.

FRANK
Nobody is looking at me.

FRANK SR.
Just tell me where you going, Frank? Somewhere exotic. Tell me where you're going?

Frank stares at his father for a long BEAT.

FRANK
Hollywood.

FRANK SR.
Hollywood. My son is going to Hollywood tonight.

Frank Sr. downs his drink.

FRANK SR.
The rest of us really are suckers.

INT. - FBI OFFICES. - WASHINGTON. - DAY
SUPER: FBI BUILDING, WASHINGTON, D.C.

CLOSE ON: A SLIDE PROJECTOR — the circular tray turning clockwise as one of Frank's checks is projected onto a free standing screen. FBI AGENT CARL HAN-RATTY stands at the front of the room addressing FIVE FBI AGENTS.

HANRATTY
John Doe 2172 is a paperhanger who started on the

East Coast. During the last few weeks, 2172 has developed a new form of check fraud, which I'm calling "the float." Next slide.

The slide doesn't change.

HANRATTY
Next slide, please.

FBI AGENT
The remote thing is broken. You'll have to do it by hand.

Carl reaches in and turns the slide.

HANRATTY
What he's doing is opening checking accounts at various banks, then changing the MICR ink routing numbers on the bottom of those checks.

CLOSE ON: The Agents listening to Carl, having no idea what he's talking about. Some of the men are yawning, while other are doodling at their desks.

HANRATTY
This is a map of the 12 banks of the U.S. Federal Reserve. The MICR scanners at the bank read the numbers on the bottom of a check — then ship the check off to the corresponding branch.

My name is Bill Rehder and I was formerly a special agent with the FBI I had a 33 year career with the bureau and spent 32 of those years in Los Angeles. I worked in the Los Angeles bank robbery squad. The last 18 years of my career, I was the so-called bank robbery coordinator, which means that I investigated and coordinated all of the bank robberies that occurred within the seven counties that encompass and surround the City of Los Angeles. I have been retired since 1999 and this has been my first opportunity to function as a technical advisor on a movie.

My job on the set was to offer advice about the authenticity of the script and on the sets, costumes, props, and the manner in which the agents conduct themselves. The depictions here are very accurate in terms of how a check passer works and what materials he needs for this type of crime.

The FBI set for the field office was so completely representative of a typical field office that I almost had to blink my eyes to make sure it wasn't real. Obviously, the filmmakers had done a lot of research because even the doorframes and the style of windows were exactly right.

As far as the day-to-day operations within a field division, I was able to tell them how things were in a typical field office. For example, when we would leave for the evening, our desks had to be cleared; everything had to be spic and span. The so-called work boxes where we stored papers were locked up each night. The bureau in the 1960s was a semi-military type of a setting. That's the way Mr. Hoover liked it.

—William J. Rehder,
FBI Technical Advisor

LEFT CENTER: *The set for the scenes filmed in the FBI offices was created from unused office space at Boeing in Downey, California, as shown center.*

65

SPECIAL AGENT WITKINS
Carl, for those of us not familiar with bank fraud, would you mind telling us what the hell you're talking about?

HANRATTY
The East Coast branches are numbered zero-one to zero-six, central is zero-seven and zero-eight....

SPECIAL AGENT WITKINS
You mean to say that those numbers on the bottom of a check actually mean something?

HANRATTY
Yes. And if you change a zero-two to a one-two — a check cashed in New York won't be sent to the New York Federal branch — but will be re-routed all the way to San Francisco. The bank won't know the check has bounced for two weeks, which means this guy can stay in one place — paper the same city over and over while his checks circle the country.

The AGENTS literally scratch their heads, trying to follow.

SPECIAL AGENT WITKINS
And this is why you called for an emergency briefing? Because of a couple of bounced checks?

Laughter from the other Agents as Carl tries to smile.

HANRATTY
Sean, I was hoping to get some back-up on this.

SPECIAL AGENT WITKINS
You want my wife to help you? She's the one who balances the checkbook at home.

INT. - RENTAL CAR. - HOLLYWOOD. - DAY
SUPER: HOLLYWOOD, CALIFORNIA - NOVEMBER, 1964

FBI AGENTS AMDURSKY AND FOX are driving with Carl through Hollywood. Fox sits in the back holding a street map.

AMDURSKY
...I'm wearing a red dress and high heels, running through this park and chasing these two Puerto Ricans with a suitcase filled with marijuana — and I reach for my radio to call for back-up, but the radio is stuck in my bra....

Carl turns up the volume on the radio, keeps his eyes on the road as he drives.

AMDURSKY
That's a funny story. People always laugh at that story.

HANRATTY
Let me ask you something, Amdursky. If you had so much fun working undercover, why did you transfer into bank fraud?

AGENT AMDURSKY
I didn't transfer. I was demoted.
(*off Carl's look*)
Demoted is the wrong word. It was more like...punished. I screwed up in the field.

HANRATTY
What about you, Mr. Fox? Did you screw up in the field and get punished?

FOX
No. I've never worked in the field before. I was a historian at the bureau's main library. We had to close because of the fire.

HANRATTY
That's really great. I ask for back-up, they drag the bottom of the Pacific.

AMDURSKY
Can I ask you something, Agent Hanratty? How come you're so serious all the time?

HANRATTY
Does it bother you?

AGENT AMDURSKY
Yes. It bothers me.

HANRATTY
Does it bother you, Mr. Fox?

FOX
A little, I guess.

HANRATTY
Would you guys like to hear me tell a joke?

AGENT AMDURSKY
Yeah. We'd love to hear a joke from you.

HANRATTY
Knock, knock.

AGENT AMDURSKY
Who's there?

HANRATTY
Go fuck yourselves.

EXT. - TROPICANA HOTEL. - HOLLYWOOD. - DAY
Frank wears a black suit and holds a box of stationary supplies as he crosses by a busy motel pool area, smiling at some of the girls in the pool as he makes his way toward the stairs that lead to his room. A YOUNG MAN is helping his BLIND FATHER slowly down the stairs, and Frank steps aside to let them pass.

Tropicana Motel

A lot of designers feel that the 1960s represented the nadir of American design to date — the loudest and craziest taste, and the ugliest buildings. I personally hadn't paid that much attention to the 1960s before taking on this project. This movie actually forced me to go back and look at what was being built and designed during that decade. It was a time when people felt a little more frivolous than they had during the '50s, a little freer to burst out and use wild colors more personally, create things for the fun of creating them. We had fun playing with some of those elements, like the sign at the Tropicana Motel for example. We struggled for a long time to find a preserved exterior motel with a wonderful sign from the late '50s or early '60s. It never happened. We finally ended up making one ourselves.

—JEANNINE OPPEWALL,
PRODUCTION DESIGNER

ABOVE: *The exterior sign for the Tropicana Motel was created for the movie at the back entrance of the legendary Roosevelt Hotel on Hollywood Boulevard.*

67

FRANK
Have a good lunch, Mr. Murphy. I'll save you a spot at the pool.

EXT. - TROPICANA MOTEL. - HOLLYWOOD. - DAY
The unmarked FBI SEDAN pulls up to TWO-STORY MOTEL on the SUNSET STRIP. Carl, Amdursky, and Fox walk into the motel office, all in black suits and sunglasses.

INT. - TROPICANA MOTEL. - HOLLYWOOD. - DAY
Hanratty, Amdursky, and Fox are standing at the front desk of the motel, where the OWNER stands in front of a fan.

MOTEL OWNER
He wrote three checks. They all cleared. I was gonna deposit this one today.

The owner takes a check out of the register, hands it to Carl.

MOTEL OWNER
I don't want any trouble.

Carl stares at the check for a BEAT, slowly starts to smile.

HANRATTY
There is no trouble. The bank called us. We'll just take this check and be on our way.

MOTEL OWNER
Good. I don't want my customers harassed.

Hanratty stares at the owner for a BEAT, the blood rushing to his face.

HANRATTY
What are you saying? He's still here? Where?

MOTEL OWNER
201.

HANRATTY
You guys stay here, watch the front.

AMDURSKY
Stay here? This guy's a pen and ink man, a goddamn paperhanger. He doesn't even carry a gun.

FOX
Why can't we go with you, Carl?

HANRATTY
Just be quiet and watch the front. And if you're good, when we're finished, I'll buy you a Good Humor bar.

Amdursky gives him a look.

HANRATTY
Relax, Earl, you'll get one too.

EXT. - TROPICANA MOTEL. - HOLLYWOOD. - DAY
Carl Hanratty walks through the busy pool area of the motel, passing a few FLIGHT ATTENDANTS who are sitting by the tiny pool. Carl makes his way up the main stairwell — walks through a fire door with his gun leading the way.

CLOSE ON: ROOM 201 at the end of the second floor hallway, the DO NOT DISTURB SIGN hanging off the door. Carl slowly makes his way down the hall, passing a MAID who is about to scream — until he shows her his badge and violently motions for her to hide inside a room.

Carl creeps along the wall, his gun straight out, his face covered in sweat. It's clear he hasn't done this much — if ever, and he looks a bit confused when he sees that the door to ROOM 201 IS AJAR. He moves his hand onto the door, and pushes it open as he throws his body into the room.

HANRATTY
FBI!

The room is empty. Hanratty slowly moves in, checks the closet — makes his way toward a small desk — stares down at an ELECTRIC TYPEWRITER. He pulls a CHECK from the carriage — holds it up to the light. There are hundreds of checks on the desk, along with glue, ink, drafting pens, and scissors.

FRANK
That's the new IBM Selectric — you can change the print type in five seconds. Just pop out the ball.

Carl turns and bumps into the chair, almost dropping his gun as he spins and faces Frank, who walks out of the bathroom wearing a black suit.

HANRATTY
Don't move! Put your hands on your head or I'll shoot!

Frank slowly walks into the room — motions to the desk.

FRANK
He's got about two hundred checks here — a gallon of Indian ink, drafting glue — he even makes little payroll envelopes addressed to himself from Pan Am.

Hanratty looks confused — his finger on the trigger as Frank makes his way toward him.

HANRATTY
Keep your hands where I can see them!

FRANK
Relax, buddy, you're late. My name is

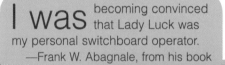

I was becoming convinced that Lady Luck was my personal switchboard operator.
—Frank W. Abagnale, from his book

Clothes Make the Man

When I first read the script, I thought, "Uh-oh, Leo's in his pilot uniform an awful lot." Then I read it again, and I realized that he had one hundred wardrobe changes! That's much more than average. I think Madonna holds the record on *Evita*, though Leo just may break that record on this movie.

Throughout the movie, his character is keenly aware of how his clothes impress other people and how crucial his appearance is to influencing others' perceptions. I think he learned that from his father. It's an important part of his character and, in that context, the number of changes makes perfect sense.

—MARY ZOPHRES, COSTUME DESIGNER

Allen, Barry Allen, United States Secret Service. Your boy just tried to climb out the window — my partner has him in custody downstairs.

HANRATTY
What are you talking about? Keep your hands up!

FRANK
You think the FBI are the only ones tracking this guy? He's been dabbling in government checks. We've been following a paper trail for months, almost had him in New York. Would you mind taking that gun out of my face, it makes me nervous.

HANRATTY
Let me see some identification.

FRANK
Here. Take my whole wallet.

Frank takes out his wallet, tosses it to Carl, who catches it with his free hand. The wallet is latched with a leather strap, and Carl is having trouble opening it with one hand.

FRANK
You want my gun, too? Come over here and take my gun.

Frank opens his jacket, but not wide enough for Carl to see that he's not armed. As Carl finally gets the wallet strap open...

FRANK
Take a look out the window — my partner is walking him toward the car. Old guy almost peed in his pants when I came through the door. Climbed right out the window onto the hood of my car.

Carl hesitates, then slowly walks toward the window and looks out — SEES THE YOUNG MAN LEADING HIS BLIND FATHER ACROSS THE STREET, HIS HANDS CLUTCHING THE OLD MAN'S ARMS AS HE WALKS HIM TOWARD A PARKED CAR.

Frank yells out the open window.

FRANK
(*yelling to the car*)
Get him in the car, Murph. And call the LAPD again — I don't want people walking through my crime scene!

Carl turns to Frank, takes a deep breath and holsters his weapon.

HANRATTY
I didn't expect Secret Service on this.

FRANK
Don't worry about it. What's your name, anyway?

HANRATTY
Hanratty, Carl.

FRANK
You mind if I see a badge? Can't be too careful these days.

HANRATTY
Sure.

Carl shows him his badge.

FRANK
Tough luck, Carl. Five minutes earlier and you would have landed yourself a pretty good collar.

HANRATTY
That's okay. Ten seconds later you would have been shot.

The two men share a quick laugh.

HANRATTY
You mind if I come downstairs and take a look at this guy.

FRANK
Sure thing. Just do me a favor, Carl, sit tight one minute while I get some of this evidence downstairs. We called the LAPD, but they're out to lunch and I'm afraid some maid is gonna walk in here and start making the bed.

Frank picks up the MICR MACHINE AND A STACK OF CHECKS, starts moving toward the open door.

HANRATTY
Wait.

Frank stops, slowly turns back to Carl.

HANRATTY
Your wallet.

FRANK
Hang onto it for a minute. I trust you.

EXT. - TROPICANA MOTEL. - HOLLYWOOD. - DAY
Frank walks downstairs, heads for the EMERGENCY EXIT.

INT. - ROOM 201. - MINUTES LATER
Carl Hanratty is standing in the middle of room 201 looking at a pile of checks. After a BEAT he looks down at the wallet in his hand, his mind starting to consider a single horrible thought. He slowly opens the wallet — takes out a thick wad of LABELS — ALL FROM BOTTLES — COCA-COLA, CHAMPAGNE, HEINZ KETCHUP, PEANUTS — EACH LABEL PERFECTLY INTACT.

Carl rushes to the window — the car is gone. A moment later Frank appears in the alley holding the MICR machine. He stares up at Carl for a BEAT, then quickly turns and walks toward Hollywood Boulevard.

INT. - FBI OFFICES. - WASHINGTON. - DAY
Carl Hanratty is sitting in the office of Special Agent Witkins.

SPECIAL AGENT WITKINS
Sometimes we all get a little lost out there, Carl. No shame in being rusty. You want to talk about it?

HANRATTY
Not really. I made a mistake.

SPECIAL AGENT WITKINS
Forget about it. There are hundreds of John Does out there.

HANRATTY
Yeah, but I'm gonna get this one. The worst thing a paperhanger can do is show his face.

SPECIAL AGENT WITKINS
I saw the report. Dark hair, six-foot-

two, 27 to 30 years old, 160 pounds. You sure this is all you remember?

HANRATTY
I saw him, Sean, I heard his voice — there's nothing for him to hide behind.

SPECIAL AGENT WITKINS
Just be careful. You've got 12 years in, nobody bothers you down on the first floor. You practically wrote the book on fraud, and that's good enough to make you Section Chief some day. There's no reason to put yourself in this type of position.

HANRATTY
What position is that?

SPECIAL AGENT WITKINS
The position of being humiliated.

Carl stares at Witkins, slowly stands and heads for the door. He's about to leave when he turns and looks back at Witkins.

HANRATTY
Hey, Sean, you want to hear a joke?

SPECIAL AGENT WITKINS
Sure.

HANRATTY
Knock, knock.

INT. - PAN AM CONFERENCE ROOM. - DAY
Paul Morgan sits across from Frank eating lunch. Frank is dressed in school clothes and holding a notebook.

FRANK
What's the altimeter supposed to read during the approach on a shallow landing?

MORGAN
Kid, I'm really not in the mood for this today. That damn Skywayman is driving me crazy. There was another article.

FRANK
Who's the Skywayman?

Morgan hands Frank a copy of the NEW YORK COURIER.

MORGAN
Some nut flying around the country posing as a Pan Am pilot. The Courier has devoted a weekly column to him.

Frank stares down at the COURIER, his eyes wide as he stares at the headline: SKYWAYMAN VISITS CALIFORNIA: ELUSIVE PHONY STILL FLYING THE FRIENDLY SKIES.

FRANK
The Skywayman...

MORGAN
I keep telling them it's not my problem. He doesn't fly on Pan Am planes — he flies on everybody else. The damn paper is in love with this clown — they call him the James Bond of the sky.

The Tom Hanks character, Carl Hanratty, is a typical example of an agent who is very, very dedicated to his work. When he is confronted and then conned by Frank Abagnale in the hotel room, Carl's reaction is to take it very personally. I can identify with that very much. Any agent who has been embarrassed to that extent would take it personally. The cool, professional attitude can slip aside when one becomes obsessed with the capture of the one who got away.

I had a partner in the Cleveland division when I first started in 1966 and he looked very much like Mr. Hanks, right down to the glasses and the fedora hat. Watching him was a real trip down memory lane for me.

—William J. Rehder,
FBI Technical Advisor

FRANK
Did you say James Bond?

INT. - MOVIE THEATER. - NIGHT
Frank is sitting in a movie theater watching GOLDFINGER, his eyes glued to the screen. He's eating a box of popcorn, a big smile on his face as he stares up at SEAN CONNERY.

INT. - NEW YORK HOTEL SUITE. - DAY
Frank is wearing a grey James Bond suit, looking at himself in a full length mirror — A SALESMAN AND A TAILOR standing behind him.

FRANK
And you're sure this is the suit?

SALESMAN
Positive. That's the same one he wore in the movie.

FRANK
Okay. I'll take three.

SALESMAN
Now all you need is one of those little foreign sports cars he drives.

EXT. - COUNTRY ROAD. - DAY
Frank is speeding along in his silver ASTON MARTIN. He pulls up behind a woman with flowing blonde hair in a red Mustang, speeds up along side and gives her his best James Bond smile. The 60-year-old woman tilts her glasses and smiles right back —

I learned early that class is universally admired. Almost any fault, sin or crime is considered more leniently if there's a touch of class involved.
—Frank W. Abagnale, from his book

INT. - FBI OFFICES. - WASHINGTON, D.C. - EVENING
CLOSE ON: A FINGERPRINT UNDER A MAGNIFYING GLASS — WE SEE ONE PRINT AFTER ANOTHER.

CARL HANRATTY is looking through a giant PRINT BOOK — tediously searching for a match. Carl is alone in the fingerprint lab, where a pathetic looking Christmas tree sits in the corner of the room. The phone rings, and Carl quickly answers.

HANRATTY (ON PHONE)
This is Hanratty. Merry Christmas.

FRANK
Hello, Carl.

Carl sits up in his chair, looks around the empty room.

HANRATTY
Barry Allen, Secret Service.

Carl grabs a pencil and searches for a piece of paper.

FRANK
I've been trying to track you down for a couple of hours.

HANRATTY
What do you want?

FRANK
I wanted to apologize for what happened out in Los Angeles.

HANRATTY
Fuck you. Don't you apologize to me.

FRANK
Carl, do you always work on Christmas Eve?

Carl looks around the room before he answers.

In the script, Frank sees the movie *Goldfinger* and then buys the same suit worn by Sean Connery. Up until that point in the script, he has only worn a suit as a chauffeur and a pilot. We screened *Goldfinger*, downloaded an image off the computer and took it to our tailor. We tried to match the fabric as closely as possible. Capturing the "look" really came down to getting the fit. You can use the best fabric and duplicate a style exactly, but if the suit isn't cut perfectly to fit the actor, it will never work.
—Mary Zophres, Costume Designer

Dressing the FBI

In the 1960s, J. Edgar Hoover was still the head of the FBI and he had a very rigid dress code. We tried to follow that code while dressing Tom Hanks' character and all the other FBI agents in the movie. Agents were required to wear dark conservative suits, white dress shirts, and ties with diagonal stripes. Hoover also dictated that no red should be in the ties (because of red's association with communism).

Tom's silhouette in the 1960s portion of the movie is very consistent. We found one or two original 1960s suits (three button, narrow lapel, single breasted) that had never been worn and fit Tom well. They became the model for all of his 1960s suits. Our tailor copied the details of this original suit exactly and I chose traditional fabrics in weights that most closely matched suits from the 1960s.

Even though Tom's character had about a dozen suits, shirts, and ties from the 1960s, they're indistinguishable. It gave a regimen to his character that was in contrast to Leonardo's, which was constantly changing.

His glasses were also key in creating his look. We tried several until we found the perfect pair. He was not Carl until he had on his glasses. Tom's short brim fedora was also essential to his overall "Carl" look.

In the 1970s, Hoover was out of office and the FBI loosened up a bit but, for Carl Hanratty, old habits die hard. He still had a very consistent silhouette, a very conservative, early '70s feel (slightly wider lapel, wider belt loops, wider collar and tie).

Again, we found a conservative 1970s suit, which became the model for the suits for the 1970s portion of the film.

—MARY ZOPHRES,
COSTUME DESIGNER

HANRATTY
I volunteered so that men with families could go home early.

FRANK
It looked like you were wearing a wedding ring in L.A. I thought maybe you had a family?

HANRATTY
No. No family.

FRANK
How come?

HANRATTY
You want to talk to me, let's talk face to face.

FRANK
Okay. I'm in my suite at Stuyvesant Arms. 3113. In the morning I'm going to Las Vegas for the weekend.

Carl starts to write this down, then suddenly stops himself.

HANRATTY
You think you're gonna get me again, don't you? You're not going to Vegas, and you're not at the Stuyvesant Arms. You'd love for me to send twenty agents out on Christmas Eve to barge into that hotel, break down doors so you can make a....

FRANK
Carl, I'm sorry if I made a fool out of you.

HANRATTY
Goddamn it, don't you feel sorry for me. The truth is, I knew it was you. Maybe I didn't pull the trigger, but I knew.

FRANK
People only know what you tell them.

HANRATTY
Then tell me something, Barry. How did you know I wouldn't look in the wallet?

FRANK
The same reason the Yankees always win. Nobody can keep their eyes off the pinstripes.

HANRATTY
The Yankees win because they have Mickey Mantle. Nobody bets on the uniform.

FRANK
Are you sure about that, Carl?

HANRATTY
No. I'm not. But I am sure you're gonna get caught. One way or another — it's a mathematical fact. Just like Vegas — the house always wins.

A BEAT OF SILENCE.

FRANK
I have to go.

HANRATTY
You didn't call to apologize, did you?

FRANK
What do you mean?

In the 1960s, agents were regimented to a certain degree. Certainly our clothes and hairstyle were all somewhat mandated by the Bureau office. Long hair was not tolerated. Beards and mustaches were not tolerated. Clothing was always very conservative business-wear. White shirts were preferred. Of course the mode of the day was a three-button suit, usually with the top two buttons buttoned and a slender tie. We did have a certain likeness, if you will, at the time. As far as the personalities were concerned, the agents were very resolute.

—William J. Rehder,
FBI Technical Advisor

HANRATTY
You've got no one else to call.

The line goes dead. Carl cups his hands to his face, then stares at a picture of his WIFE AND FOUR-YEAR-OLD DAUGHTER — which sits on the desk in front of him.

INT. - STUYVESANT ARMS HOTEL SUITE. - EVENING
Frank slowly hangs up the phone. He walks over to the chair in the room, picks up his Pilot's Cap and puts it on. As he walks out the door, WE SEE THE SUITE NUMBER — 3113.

INT. - FBI OFFICES. - WASHINGTON D.C. - DAY
Carl Hanratty looks extremely tense as he uses a slide projector to file a report in front of TEN AGENTS.

HANRATTY
I'm calling it "The Switch." Next slide.

The slide doesn't change.

HANRATTY
Next slide!

FBI AGENT
You have to hit the thing on the side a few times.

Carl hits the slide projector, and the slide changes.

HANRATTY
On December 28, John Doe 2172 took 250 deposit slips from Nevada Savings and Loan and encoded his account number on the bottom of each one. He then placed the checks on the counter for other customers to use.

SPECIAL AGENT WITKINS
Wait a second, Carl. Those slips don't even have his name on them.

HANRATTY
The bank scanners read the MICR ink before they read pen ink. So even though those deposit slips were filled out correctly, each customer who made a deposit that day was actually putting money into his account.

SPECIAL AGENT WITKINS
How much did he get?

HANRATTY
Forty-six thousand, four hundred and twelve dollars. It was the second largest bank robbery in the history of Las Vegas.

The Agents stare up at Carl, still a bit confused.

HANRATTY
What did we get back on Barry Allen?

FOX
So far we've got 618 Barry Allens over the age of 25, but that doesn't include numbers from Utah and Vermont.

HANRATTY
Let's start going down the list. I want a state by state search of every Barry Allen who's ever committed a crime, gotten a traffic ticket, bounced a check. I know it's not his real name, but it's the name he chose — and I want to know why.

INT. HALLWAY. - HOTEL. - NIGHT
Frank wears a black suit as he walks down a hallway — passing a STUNNING BRUNETTE wearing an evening gown and holding a glass of champagne. As Frank is opening the door to his room, the brunette is opening the door to her room.

I play a very high-class hooker with a heart. I'm a bad girl Jackie O.

We shot my scenes at the Ambassador Hotel in downtown Los Angeles, which used to be this beautiful place where all the movie stars stayed. I think Frank Sinatra stayed in one of the bungalows. And, of course, this is where Bobby Kennedy was shot. There are two different places in the hotel where people will tell you that happened. I don't know which one is correct but I've worked here before. On *Alias* we used this hotel for some scenes in Cuba.

—Jennifer Garner

FRANK
Hi.

The woman smiles at Frank, is about to walk into her room.

FRANK
I've seen you before, haven't I?

CHERYL
Maybe. A couple of years ago I was on the cover of *Vogue*.
And *Cosmo*.

Frank slowly walks toward her, can barely contain his excitement.

FRANK
You're that model. Cheryl Ann! Guys used to put your picture in their lockers!

CHERYL
Isn't that your silver car I saw parked out front?

FRANK
Yeah. One of them. Do you think I could get an autograph some time?

Cheryl turns to Frank.

CHERYL
Do you have a pen in your room?

Frank can't help but smile.

FRANK
Cheryl Ann...I got lots of pens.

INT. LAUNDROMAT. - NIGHT.
CLOSE ON: An old washing machine spinning — slightly off balance.

Carl Hanratty sits on top of a dryer wearing his black suit — his hat off as he stares at his whites as they turn in the machine. In his hand is a computer print out — the name BARRY ALLEN written over and over.

The washing machine suddenly stops, and Carl walks over and opens the glass door — slowly pulls out a single white undershirt — which has been dyed pink. He yanks out the rest of the load — it's all pink — every last sock.

HANRATTY
Son of a...

Carl reaches deep into the machine, pulls out a red string bikini top — which someone had obviously left in the machine.

INT. FRANK'S HOTEL SUITE. - NIGHT
Frank and Cheryl are slow dancing in the middle of the Suite. They start to kiss, and Cheryl slowly pulls away. She walks over to a desk and picks up a DECK OF CARDS that have the HOTEL SEAL on the front. Cheryl starts tossing cards onto the bed.

CHERYL
A man like you can buy anything he wants, and he buys a deck of cards in the hotel gift shop.

FRANK
You want to see a card trick?

CHERYL
How much did these cards cost?

FRANK
Fifty-five cents.

CHERYL
And if they sold me downstairs in the hotel gift shop, how much
would you pay?

FRANK
How much would I pay for what?

CHERYL
The entire night. How much would you pay me for the entire night?

Frank stares at her, suddenly realizes what
she's saying.

FRANK
I really don't know.

CHERYL
Don't be scared. Make me an offer.

Frank hesitates for a long BEAT.

FRANK
Three hundred.

CHERYL
Go fish.

FRANK
Six hundred.

CHERYL
Go fish.

FRANK
One thousand dollars.

CHERYL
Okay. A thousand dollars.

Frank reaches into his pocket as he walks
toward the door.

FRANK
I'll be right back.

CHERYL
Wait a second. Where are you going?

FRANK
I'm going downstairs to cash a check.

CHERYL
You think this hotel is going to cash a thousand dollar
check at 3 A.M.?

Frank holds up one of his CHECKS.

FRANK
This is a check from New York Savings and Loan. Just like gold —
they'll cash it.

CHERYL
Don't you think they might get a little suspicious? Let me see that
check.

Frank shows her the check, and she studies it.

CHERYL
This is a cashier's check — just endorse it over to me.

I had established and followed a certain felonious code of ethics since taking up crime as a profession. Among other things, I'd never diddled an individual. For instance, I'd never purchased a wardrobe or any other personal item with a hot check. Too many department stores and business firms held an individual salesperson responsible for bogus checks. If a salesman took a check for a suit, and the check bounced, the cost of the suit came out of the clerk's salary. My targets had always been corporate targets — banks, airlines, hotels, motels, or other establishments protected by insurance. When I splurged on a new wardrobe or anything else of a personal nature, I always hit a bank or a hotel for the needed cash.

It suddenly occurred to me that Cheryl would make a lovely exception to my rule.

—Frank W. Abagnale, from his book

FRANK
I couldn't do that. This check is for $1400. We already agreed on a thousand.

Cheryl stares at Frank for a BEAT, reaches into her bra and takes out FOUR HUNDRED DOLLARS.

CHERYL
I'll give you back $400. You give me the check.

She hands Frank the cash, takes the check from his hand.

FRANK
Even better.

INT. - COFFEE SHOP. - DAY

Carl Hanratty looks exhausted as he sits alone in a quiet coffee shop. He's staring down at an old fashioned computer printout — 20 pages of big block letters giving the address of every BARRY ALLEN in the country.

A SIXTEEN-YEAR-OLD WAITER walks over with a pot of coffee.

YOUNG WAITER
More coffee, Sir?

HANRATTY
Sure.

As he pours the coffee, the waiter glances at the printout.

YOUNG WAITER
You a collector?

HANRATTY
Excuse me?

YOUNG WAITER
"Captives of the Cosmic Ray." "The Big Freeze." "Land of the Golden Giants." I've got them all.

HANRATTY
I don't understand.

The waiter motions to the napkin.

YOUNG WAITER
Barry Allen.

Hanratty looks confused as he stares up at the waiter.

YOUNG WAITER
The Flash.

EXT. - WASHINGTON D.C. - PAY PHONE. - AFTER-NOON

Carl holds an open "FLASH" COMIC BOOK in his hand — the name BARRY ALLEN bubbled over the face of a YOUNG BOY just before he turns into a superhero. A light rain falls as Carl talks on the phone.

HANRATTY
Comic books — he reads comic books. Barry Allen is The Flash!

FOX (V.O.)
(*through phone*)
Carl, slow down. I don't know what the hell you're talking about.

HANRATTY
He's a kid — the unsub is a kid. That's why we can't match his prints — that's why he has no record. I want you to call the NYPD, get every all-points

for juvenile runaways in New York City. And don't forget the airports, he's been kiting checks all over the country.

FOX (V.O.)
(*through phone*)
Why New York?

HANRATTY
He said something about the Yankees.

FOX (V.O.)
(*through phone*)
Jesus, Carl, there's gonna be thousands of kids on that list.

HANRATTY
Find out if any of them ever bounced a check.

EXT. - PAULA ABAGNALE'S HOME. - LONG ISLAND. - DAY
Carl Hanratty, holding a list in his hands, wearing a black hat and black overcoat, is knocking on the door with Amdursky and Fox.

FOX
What number is this?

HANRATTY
Fifty-three. Abagnale.

Paula answers with a cigarette in her hand.

HANRATTY
Good morning, ma'am, we're the FBI Agents who called.

PAULA
Yes. I've been waiting. I hope you're all hungry. I put out the Sara Lee.

INT. - PAULA'S HOME. - LONG ISLAND. - DAY
Paula sits on the living room couch pouring three cups of coffee. There is a plate of CAKE on the table in front of her, and she's slicing it for the Agents.

PAULA
My husband Jack is a lawyer.

Paula motions to a FRAMED PICTURE of Jack Barnes.

HANRATTY
And your first husband? It says here you were recently divorced from Frank William Abagnale.

PAULA
Why can't you people leave Frank alone? He's a veteran — a medal of honor winner...

HANRATTY
So you met him during the war?

PAULA
I lived in a very small village in France. The kind of place where they've never heard of Sara Lee. Now who wants a piece?

Amdursky holds up his hand.

AMDURSKY
Nobody doesn't like Sara Lee.

Hanratty gives him a look.

HANRATTY
Ma'am, you filed a police report for a juvenile runaway named Frank Abagnale Jr.

Carl hands her a copy of the police report.

PAULA
Is Frankie okay?

HANRATTY
You're aware of the fact that your son wrote some checks on a closed account at Chase Manhattan Bank?

PAULA
Yes. The police think he's some type of criminal.

HANRATTY
What he did was a felony.

PAULA
It was a thousand dollars.
(*lights a cigarette*)
Half the kids his age are on dope, throwing rocks at police, and they scared me to death because my son made a little mistake. A seventeen-year-old boy has to eat, has to have a place to sleep. He's a baby, what do you want him to do?

HANRATTY
I understand, ma'am. Do you have a picture of your son?

PAULA
Yes. I have his old yearbook.

Paula walks over to a table, opens the WESTBOURNE HIGH SCHOOL YEARBOOK to a page marked SOPHOMORES. She points to tiny black and white picture of Frank wearing a coat and tie. Carl stares down at the picture for a long BEAT, then slowly turns to Fox and Amdursky.

HANRATTY
We need to send a telex. Our unsub is named Frank Abagnale Jr., and he's 17.

The three agents quickly stand and walk toward the door.

PAULA
Is Frankie okay. Is he in trouble?

HANRATTY
Ma'am, I'm sorry to have to tell you that your son is forging checks.

PAULA
Forging checks? Wait, I'm sure we can take care of that. I'm working part-time at the Church now. Just tell me how much he owes and I'll pay you back.

Paula takes out her CHECKBOOK.

HANRATTY
So far it's about a million dollars.

EXT. - JFK AIRPORT. - DAY
Frank is wearing his pilot's uniform as he pulls up to the airport in a German sports car. He parks the car and jumps out of the convertible, leaving the keys in the ignition.

There is enchantment in a uniform, especially one that marks the wearer as a person of rare skills, courage or achievement. . . . [My] uniform was my alter ego. I used it in the same manner a junkie shoots up on heroin. Whenever I felt lonely, depressed, rejected or doubtful of my own worth, I'd dress up in my pilot's uniform and seek out a crowd. The uniform brought me respect and dignity. Without it on, at times, I felt useless and dejected.
—Frank W. Abagnale, from his book

JFK Airport

One of our greatest coups began when we heard that Eero Saarinen's TWA terminal at JFK airport was closing. American Airlines had taken over TWA and the terminal was too small for them. There it stood, empty. New York welcomed us to use it.

The terminal is a special place for me because I used to work for Charles Eames, who was best friends with Eero Saarinen, the designer of the terminal. I did my best, within our limited time frame and budget, to restore the terminal to the way it looked in the archival photographs from the time. I hope that Eero Saarinen won't visit me in my dreams if I didn't get it exactly perfect.

—JEANNINE OPPEWALL,
PRODUCTION DESIGNER

THIS PAGE: Eero Saarinen's design for the TWA terminal is considered one of the seminal works of modern architecture. Production designer Jeannine Oppewall transformed the abandoned terminal (ABOVE) into the bustling 1960s airport seen in the film (BELOW).

INT. - JFK AIRPORT. - DAY

Frank is walking through the airport, eyeing several UNIFORMED COPS who are scattered throughout the terminal, all holding the yearbook picture of FRANK. Frank sees FOUR UNDERCOVER COPS walking toward him, then sees TWO DETECTIVES checking the identification of a PAN AM PILOT. He ducks into the AIRPORT GIFT SHOP, hides behind a magazine rack.

> **FRANK (V.O.)**
> Dear Dad. I'm no longer an airline pilot for Pan Am. I'm now an FBI Agent working undercover for the United States government.

Frank is staring at the cover of PLAYBOY MAGAZINE. He leans in as he reads the headline: RIVERBEND — THE BEST SINGLES COMPLEX IN AMERICA. He opens the magazine to a three page pull-out — and smiles as he stares down at the photograph of Riverbend.

EXT. - RIVERBEND APARTMENT COMPLEX. - ATLANTA. - DAY

SUPER: ATLANTA, GEORGIA - MAY 1965

A sprawling APARTMENT COMPLEX that lines a picturesque golf course.

There are two swimming pools, tennis courts, but most of all — WOMEN. Everywhere you look, there are women walking the grounds, swimming, playing tennis.

Frank is carrying the MICR MACHINE and a FONDUE POT into his apartment, passing TWO WOMEN in bikinis.

> **FRANK**
> Hello, ladies. I see the tomatoes are ripe this afternoon.

> **WOMAN #1**
> Where's the party tonight, Frank?

> **FRANK**
> I'm doing fondue at my place.

INT. - FRANK'S APARTMENT. - DAY

CLOSE ON: A bubbling FONDUE POT with skewers lining the rim. The PENTHOUSE APARTMENT has been transformed into a smaller version of the Playboy mansion, with young men and women smoking pot, drinking wine, and eating fondue. The place is a mess, with bottles and bodies all over the place.

Frank wears a brown suit as he navigates his way through the apartment holding a case of champagne.

> **WOMAN**
> Frank, this is great fondue. Hurry up with that champagne.

> **FRANK**
> Could you please use an ashtray, Melanie.

Frank sets the champagne down, pushes through the crowd of people, picking up bottles and plates, looking somewhat out of place in his own apartment.

Here again, a specific scene from *Goldfinger* was the reference for Leo's costume. Sean Connery is lying out in the sun and then puts on this little blue terrycloth après-sun suit. We made that outfit for Leo and he wears it by the pool just after he moves into the Riverbend apartments. Anybody who knows *Goldfinger* well enough will recognize Leo's outfit as homage to Sean Connery's poolside suit.

—Mary Zophres, Costume Designer

FRANK
James, please don't touch the phonograph system! It's reel-to-reel
— you can't wind it like that.

As Frank rushes toward the phonograph, a MAN spills a glass of wine
on his suit.

FRANK
Watch it, Terry. This is a $400 Manhattan Eagle.

TERRY
It's just a suit, man. Take it easy.

A drunk WOMAN runs in from the other room.

WOMAN
Frank, come quick. Lance just fell into the conversation pit.

INT. - ATLANTA GENERAL HOSPITAL. - ATLANTA. - NIGHT
Frank rushes through the hospital, makes his way toward a RECEPTION
DESK, where a YOUNG DOCTOR is yelling at BRENDA STRONG,
17, a thin, awkward-looking candy striper with her hair in a bun and
braces on her bottom teeth.

YOUNG DOCTOR
These bottles need to be labeled when you pick them up. Do you
understand how dangerous this is? Don't stand there crying, just
nod your head and tell me you won't do it again!

Brenda nods her head, quickly walks
away from the Doctor and sits behind the
RECEPTION DESK. She buries her head
and starts to write a letter, her body still
sobbing as Frank walks up to her.

The inspiration for the "look"
of Riverbend was twelve
months of *Playboy* magazines from
1964. Poring over each issue I found
ideas for hair, make-up, and wardrobe.
—Mary Zophres, Costume Designer

FRANK
Are you okay?

Brenda looks up at Frank, her eyes and nose puffy from crying. She covers her mouth when she talks.

BRENDA
He told me to pick up the blood, so I did. He never told me to label it.

FRANK
It's okay. What's your name?

BRENDA
Brenda.

FRANK
Brenda, I wouldn't worry about it. These Doctors don't know everything.

BRENDA
It's my first week. I think they're going to fire me.

FRANK
No. Nobody will fire you. I'll bet you're good at your job.

BRENDA
No, I'm not.

FRANK
I'll bet if I asked you to check the status of my friend, Lance Applebaum, you could do that in a second.

Brenda grabs a chart, starts to read it out loud.

BRENDA
Mr. Applebaum fractured his ankle. Doctor Ashland is treating him in exam seven.

FRANK
See that. No problem.

Brenda smiles, covering her mouth.

BRENDA
This is the emergency chart. See the blue star, that means the patient has been diagnosed. After he's treated, we put a red circle here.

FRANK
How do you like those braces?

Brenda looks embarrassed as she stares at Frank.

BRENDA
I guess they're okay.

FRANK
I got mine off last year.

Frank smiles wide, showing Brenda his teeth.

FRANK
Mine were bottoms. I hated them. I still have my mouth guard.

BRENDA
You have really nice teeth.

There was something so appealing about this early jet-set age—the Boeing 707s and Pan Am World Airways, the James Bond movies, and *Playboy* magazine. This was a time when people actually wore a suit and tie when they traveled. They got dressed up to go to Las Vegas. Nobody does that any more. Now it's sandals, shorts, and fanny packs everywhere you go.

Certainly, in my youth, this period was the epitome of glamour. Colors looked cooler then, everything was very bold and very, very stylish. It was a time of the Beatles and the Dave Clark Five and this whole brand new way of melding rock and roll music and media images that really did permeate society.

Gig style made even check forgery a cool thing.

—Tom Hanks

FRANK
And you have a pretty smile.

Brenda tries not to smile, shaking her head and covering her face.

FRANK
I'm serious. I think those braces look really good on you.

Brenda starts to blush as she continues to write her letter.

FRANK
What are you writing?

BRENDA
A letter to Ringo.

FRANK
What does it say?

BRENDA
I can't tell you. I'm embarrassed.

FRANK
Come on. What does it say?

BRENDA
It says I love him. Pretty stupid, right. Ringo Starr is never going to read my letter.

Frank stares at Brenda, starts to smile as she puts her letter in a drawer.

FRANK
Brenda, do you know if they're hiring here at the hospital?

BRENDA
I'm not sure. What do you want to do?

FRANK
I'm a doctor.

INT. - VICTOR GRIFFITH'S OFFICE. - HOSPITAL. - DAY
Frank is sitting across from VICTOR GRIFFITH, 60s, the HOSPITAL ADMINISTRATOR, who is reading over a RÉSUMÉ.

DOCTOR GRIFFITH
Harvard Medical School, top of your class, Southern California Children's Hospital. A pretty impressive resume, Doctor Conners? Why do you want to work here?

FRANK
I came to Atlanta to relax, to get away from my practice for a year. But to be honest, I think I'm a little old for Riverbend.

DOCTOR GRIFFITH
Unfortunately, the only thing I need is an emergency room supervisor for my midnight to eight shift, someone to baby-sit six interns and 20 nurses. But I doubt you'd be interested in that.

FRANK
In the past, they've always let me pick my own nurses.

INT. - FRANK'S APARTMENT. - RIVERBEND. - NIGHT
Ten people are partying in the living room.

INT. - FRANK'S BEDROOM
Frank is lying on his bed making a phony
MEDICAL SCHOOL DIPLOMA. He's using
a HARVARD BROCHURE to guide him as
he carefully places the STICK-ON letters on
the aged paper. A MAN AND WOMAN walk
into the bedroom, fall back on Frank's bed
and start to make out. Frank turns to them.

> **FRANK**
> Do either of you know any Latin?

INT. - VICTOR GRIFFITH'S OFFICE. - DAY
Frank is sitting in front of GRIFFITH and
FIVE DOCTORS, all of whom are looking
over FRANK'S FILE, which consists of the
fake HARVARD MEDICAL SCHOOL
DIPLOMA — fake letters of recommenda-
tion from SOUTHERN CALIFORNIA CHIL-
DREN'S HOSPITAL, and a fake CALIFOR-
NIA MEDICAL LICENSE.

> **DOCTOR GRIFFITH**
> Doctor Conners, here is your temporary license,
> which allows you to practice medicine in the state
> of Georgia for up to one year. And now let me be
> the first to say, welcome to Atlanta General.

ABOVE: *During a break in filming, director Steven Spielberg talks with Jeffrey Katzenberg, one of his partners in DreamWorks SKG.*

INT. - HOSPITAL. - NIGHT
Frank is standing in front of the 30 CANDY
STRIPERS, NURSES, and INTERNS who will be
working under him during the night shift. He wears
Doctor's whites, holds a clipboard as he takes roll.

> **FRANK**
> Brenda Strong?

He smiles at Brenda, who covers her mouth as she smiles back.

> **BRENDA**
> Here.

> **FRANK**
> Doctor Paul Ashland.

> **DOCTOR ASHLAND**
> Doctor Conners... will you be taking role every night?

> **FRANK**
> Yes. And if you're going to be late, I suggest you bring a note.

INT. - HOSPITAL CORRIDOR. - NIGHT
Frank walks down along hospital corridor holding his clipboard,
passing several NURSES in the hall.

> **NURSE**
> (*flirting*)
> Good evening, Doctor Conners.

> **FRANK**
> Button your uniform, Nurse Carlin. I can see your bra strap.
> This is a hospital, not a sorority.

INT. - FRANK'S APARTMENT. - DAY
ON A BLACK AND WHITE TV, DR. KILDARE tends to a burnt child
with DOCTOR GILLESPIE. He hands a specimen to a NURSE.

> **DR. KILDARE (ON TV)**
> Take this to the lab. Hemoglobin and Hematocrit. Type and
> crossmatch.

91

DR. GILLESPIE (ON TV)
Thirty milligrams of codeine every four hours. Run the plasma at 60 drops per minute until we calculate the fluid requirements. What do you estimate the degree and extent of the burns, Kildare?

Frank sits alone in his apartment eating popcorn and watching DR. KILDARE on TV.

DR. KILDARE (ON TV)
Second and third degree burns over about 20 percent of the body's surface.

DR. GILLESPIE (ON TV)
I concur. That's critical. Let's get him up to pediatrics.

INT. - FRANK'S OFFICE. - HOSPITAL. - NIGHT
The name on the office door reads FRANK CONNERS, M.D. Frank sits at his desk in front of a brand new IBM ELECTRIC TYPEWRITER. Brenda walks in holding a clipboard.

BRENDA
Doctor Conners, you need to sign these.

Brenda walks in and hands him the clipboard. Frank starts to scribble on the charts, the way Doctor's scribble out prescriptions.

BRENDA
Do you notice anything different about me, Doctor Conners?

Brenda smiles, but doesn't cover her mouth.

FRANK
You got your braces off! Let me see.

Frank moves toward her, stares at her bottom teeth.

BRENDA
I kept trying to show you all night.

FRANK
Did it hurt when they took them off? Mine felt so weird after.

BRENDA
I keep rubbing my tongue over them. I can't stop. It's so slippery.

FRANK
It feels good, doesn't it?

We were not set on casting an unknown for Brenda, although we knew we had the opportunity because we had so many big names in the film. Steven saw a tape of Amy reading for the part and that was it, we didn't look any further.

She is a very pivotal character in Frank's story. The great irony of her character is that she is the one true relationship Frank finds, but he meets her through deception. Their relationship is the tragic center of the movie. Frank finds something pure, but the foundation of the relationship is a lie. We needed an actress who could project that kind of innocence and purity.

—Walter F. Parkes and
Laurie MacDonald, Producers

BRENDA
Yes. It feels incredible.

Frank leans toward Brenda, gently starts to kiss her. As the passion increases WE HEAR the HOSPITAL P.A. SYSTEM.

P.A. OPERATOR (V.O.)
Doctor Conners, please come to Emergency. Doctor Conners to Emergency.

Frank continues to kiss Brenda.

BRENDA
Shouldn't you go?

FRANK
There's a staff Doctor in the emergency ward.

BRENDA
What if he's in surgery?

FRANK
Do you really think I have to go?

INT. - HOSPITAL HALLWAY. - NIGHT
Frank nervously paces in the hallway, taking deep breaths as he tries to calm down.

INT. - EMERGENCY WARD. - NIGHT
The elevator doors open, and Frank slowly walks into the EMERGENCY WARD, where Nurses are rushing toward a closed curtain.

EMERGENCY NURSE
In here, Doctor Conners.

Frank walks toward a closed curtain, stands in front of a bed and forces himself to look. He sees a blood, splattered sheet and three young INTERNS standing over the leg of an ELEVEN-YEAR-OLD BOY.

FRANK
Well, what do we have here?

DOCTOR ASHLAND
Bicycle accident. A fracture of the tibia, about five inches below the patella.

Frank stares at the boy's face, trying not to look at the open wound.

FRANK
Doctor Harris, do you concur?

DOCTOR HARRIS
Concur with what, Sir?

FRANK
What Doctor Ashland just said.

DOCTOR HARRIS
(confused)
Well, it was a bicycle accident. The boy told us.

FRANK
So you concur?

I never really pre-meditated anything. I would just fall into situations. For example, becoming a doctor was totally serendipitous.

I decided to move into a very swank singles complex called the Riverbend Apartments. The application for the lease asked for your occupation. I started to write "airline pilot" but noticed that the next questions asked for your employer and your supervisor's name and phone number. I realized I'd have to invent something on the spot that couldn't be checked out. I also had to justify why I drove an expensive car and wore expensive clothes but didn't go to work everyday. I wrote down the word "doctor" without giving it another thought.

The landlord asked, "What type of medical doctor are you?"

I figured that since this was a singles complex, a pediatrician would be pretty safe, so I moved in as Dr. Frank Williams, pediatrician. Everybody called me "Doc."

Once in awhile, one of the guys would come over and say, "Hey, doc, look at my leg, I don't know what I did to it." I'd say, "I can't. You need to go to your own doctor and have him look at that."

Of course, if a beautiful girl came by, I always gave her a thorough examination before sending her on her way.

I was young but not stupid.

—Frank W. Abagnale, on the movie

DOCTOR HARRIS
Well, I'm not sure we can...

DOCTOR ASHLAND
I think we should take an X ray, then stitch him up and put him in a walking cast.

FRANK
Very good, Doctor Ashland. You don't seem to have much need for me. Carry on.

Frank walks out, and Doctor Harris shakes his head, clearly upset.

DOCTOR HARRIS
I blew it, didn't I? Why didn't I concur? I panicked!

INT. - HOSPITAL JANITOR'S CLOSET. - NIGHT
Frank walks into the JANITOR'S CLOSET, steps into an empty stall and immediately starts to throw up.

INT. - FRANK'S APARTMENT. - RIVERBEND. - DAY
Frank is writing a letter at his electric typewriter. He pulls it out and reads it over, then takes out a pen and signs the name RINGO STARR.

INT. - HOSPITAL. - NIGHT
Brenda is running through the halls holding the letter.

BRENDA
He wrote me back. Ringo wrote me back from Liverpool! Doctor Conners, come quick! I got a letter from Ringo Starr, he signed his name and said I was his biggest fan!

EXT. - FRANK SR.'S EASTCHESTER APARTMENT. - DAY
Carl Hanratty is eating a slice of pizza as he talks with the LAND-LORD of the apartment building.

HANRATTY
I just need to go inside and take a quick look around?

LANDLORD
Actually, I've already evicted him for nonpayment of rent. I'm just giving him a few days to clear out his things.
(*hands him the key*)
So, search all you want. But if you find any money in there, it belongs to me.

INT. - FRANK SR.'S EASTCHESTER APARTMENT. - DAY
Carl Hanratty is walking through a one room apartment that has a hot plate and no bathroom. There are BOXES of drafting paper, envelopes, and other STATIONERY SUPPLIES pushed against the walls.

Carl starts opening drawers, searching the apartment. He stops when he finds a black and white picture of Paula and Frank Sr. sitting on the front of a U.S. ARMY TRUCK.

Carl takes Frank Sr.'s BLACK BRIEFCASE off the shelf and tries to open it. As he starts to pick the lock...

FRANK SR.
I lost the key for that.

Frank Sr. stands at the door to his apartment holding a small bag of groceries and a newspaper. There's an open bottle of whiskey in the bag, and Frank Sr. sets it on the table.

FRANK SR.
My landlord said you were a cop. But you're not a cop, are you?

Carl Hanratty puts the briefcase down, turns to Frank Sr.

HANRATTY
I'm Special Agent Hanratty with the FBI.

FRANK SR.
If you're going to arrest me, I'd like to put on a different suit.

HANRATTY
I'm not here to arrest you. I'm looking for your son — he's in trouble. Do you know where he is?

FRANK SR.
If I tell you where he is, will you promise not to tell his mother?

Carl nods.

FRANK SR.
(*lowering his voice*)
Frank made up a fake I.D. and enlisted in the Marine Corps — he's over in Vietnam right now. That kid is halfway around the world crawling through the jungle and fighting the damn communists. So don't come to my home and call my boy a criminal, because that kid has more guts than you will ever know!

HANRATTY
I never said he was a criminal, Mr. Abagnale. I said he was in trouble.

Carl turns and heads for the door.

HANRATTY
You can give me a call if you want to talk. I'll leave you my card.

As Carl drops his card on a cluttered table filled with unpaid bills, his eye focus on a POSTCARD — RHETT BUTLER AND SCARLET O'HARA IN A DRAMATIC POSE

FRANK SR.
You're not a father, are you?

HANRATTY
What?

FRANK SR.
If you were a father, you would know that I would never give up
my son.

EXT. - EASTCHESTER PHONE BOOTH. - DAY

Carl is inside a phone booth, dropping dimes into the slot.

HANRATTY
(*on phone*)
Riverbend Apartments, Sean — 415 Landover — Atlanta, Georgia!
I'm on my way to the airport right now — I'll meet the team in four
hours! Shit, I'm running out of dimes!

SEAN (V.O.)
(*through phone*)
Carl, it doesn't make sense. He's on the run. Why would he write
down his address?

HANRATTY
Because he's not running from his dad.

INT. - FRANK'S APARTMENT. - RIVERBEND. - DAY

Frank and Brenda are lying in bed together, staring at each other in the
ceiling mirrors.

FRANK
It's okay. You don't have to cry.

BRENDA
I'm sorry, I just can't do this.

FRANK
Brenda, it's okay. I don't care about you being a virgin. I can wait.

BRENDA
I want to sleep with you. I really do.

Brenda sits up, starts getting dressed.

BRENDA
I haven't told you the truth. I'm not a virgin. I had an abortion two
years ago. My parents had a friend do it — a man my father plays
golf with. Then when I got better they kicked me out of the house.

Brenda covers her face with a pillow, starts to cry.

BRENDA
I had an abortion, and they said I wasn't their daughter anymore.

FRANK
It's okay.

BRENDA
Then a few months ago they apologized and said I was their daughter, but I couldn't come home for awhile. I'm so sorry, Frank, please
don't be mad.

FRANK
Do you want me to talk to your parents? Maybe I could straighten
things out.

BRENDA
I ask them all the time, but they won't let me come home yet. My
Dad's a lawyer, and he and I have this contract. He calls it a verbal
agreement.

FRANK
What if you were engaged to a doctor, would that change anything?

Brenda removes the pillow from her face, stares at Frank.

BRENDA
What?

Two Different Worlds

We were really shooting two different worlds. One was the traditional world of the FBI guys who dress poorly, eat bad food, and drink bad coffee. This is juxtaposed to Leo who lives this glamorous life of a young playboy — spending money, staying in the best hotels, and always surrounded by beautiful women.

It's always interesting to play with two different worlds. Here the FBI world is bleak and blue— kind of unified and dull— but Leo's world is more colorful and certainly more fun. I think that's why you forgive him for stealing the six million dollars. He did it in such a naive, innocent way and he had such a good time doing it.

—JANUSZ KAMINSKI,
DIRECTOR OF PHOTOGRAPHY

LEFT: *Leonardo DiCaprio and Janusz Kaminski, the director of photography, during a break in filming the scenes that take place at the Miami airport.*

FRANK
What if I went to your parents, spoke to your father and asked his permission to marry you?

BRENDA
Don't tease me, Frank.

FRANK
I'm not teasing.

BRENDA
You would go home with me to New Orleans?

FRANK
We can leave right now.

BRENDA
Please stop teasing me.

FRANK
Brenda, we could run away together. We could run away tonight.

BRENDA
I don't understand, Frank. What are we running from?

INT. - RIVERBEND APARTMENT COMPLEX. - ATLANTA. - AFTENOON
FIVE FBI AGENTS burst through the doors of Frank's apartment. Carl Hanratty is out front, leading the men inside with his guns drawn.

FBI AGENT
We're clear. It's empty.

There's a fondue pot in the kitchen, bean bag chairs in the living room.

Carl walks over to the wall — stares at the framed HARVARD MEDICAL SCHOOL DIPLOMA.

INT. - HOSPITAL. - NIGHT

Carl Hanratty is leading a small army of cops down a hallway, holding the Harvard Diploma in his hand. They make their way to the front of a door marked: FRANK CONNERS, M.D.

> **HANRATTY**
> Kick it in.

The Agents kick down the door, and Hanratty walks into the office, stares at an electric typewriter that is humming on the desk.

INT. - FILE CABINET. - HOSPITAL. — NIGHT

Dr. Griffith is pulling open a massive file drawer, searching through the files.

> **HANRATTY**
> What's her name?

> **DOCTOR GRIFFITH**
> We have very strict rules which prohibit doctors from any personal...

> **HANRATTY**
> He wasn't a doctor. Just tell me her name. Where was she from?

> **DOCTOR GRIFFITH**
> They come and go — mostly high school dropouts. She had only been here a few months. Brenda Strong.

Dr. Griffith opens a file marked BRENDA STRONG.

> **HANRATTY**
> What's wrong?

> **DOCTOR GRIFFITH**
> That's peculiar. Her file is empty.

EXT. - BRENDA'S PARENTS HOUSE. - NEW ORLEANS. - EVENING

A WHITE CADILLAC is parked in the driveway of a large, two-story house.

INT. BRENDA'S PARENTS HOUSE - EVENING

Frank, dressed in a plain white suit, sits at the dinner table with Brenda and her parents, ROGER and CAROL STRONG. The house is old and warm, the table jammed with food.

> **CAROL**
> Doctor Conners, are you a Lutheran?

> **FRANK**
> Yes, Ma'am. I'm a Lutheran. And please, call me Frank.

> **ROGER**
> Frank, would you like to say grace?

> Frank stares at Brenda and her parents, who bow their heads. He hesitates for a BEAT, and WE SEE that he has no idea how to say grace. After a BEAT Roger lifts his head.

> **ROGER**
> Unless you're not comfortable.

> Brenda peeks at Frank, who closes his eyes and bows his head.

> **FRANK**
> Two little mice fell in a bucket of cream. The first mouse gave up and drowned, but the second mouse struggled so hard that he churned that cream into butter — and he walked out. Amen.

I think the movie is about youthful deception and how vulnerable we are to youth and beauty. The most amazing part about this true story is Frank's age when he got away with his deceptions.
—Martin Sheen

They all lift their heads, clearly impressed. Carol turns to Frank and smiles.

CAROL
Amen. That was beautiful.

Brenda grabs Frank's hand, holds onto him for dear life.

CAROL
Frank, have you decided which hospital you want to work at here in New Orleans?

FRANK
To be honest, I've been thinking about getting back into law.

ROGER
What do you mean? Are you a doctor or a lawyer?

FRANK
Before I went to medical school I passed the bar in California. I practiced law for a year, then decided to try my hand at pediatrics.

CAROL
Oh my, a doctor and a lawyer. I'd say Brenda hit the jackpot.

ROGER
Where did you go to law school?

FRANK
Berkeley.

BRENDA
Berkeley? Isn't that where you went, Daddy?

CAROL
Maybe Frank could come work for you, Roger. You're always saying how hard it is to find Assistant Prosecutors.

BRENDA
Could he, Dad? Could Frank work for you?

Roger stares at Frank for a BEAT.

ROGER
Was that snake Hollingsworth still teaching when you went through Berkeley?

FRANK
Yes, Sir. Grumpy old Hollingsworth. Meaner than ever.

ROGER
And that dog of his? Tell me, Frank, what was the name of his little dog?

Everyone stares at Frank now, waiting.

FRANK
I'm sorry, Sir. The dog was dead.

INT. - BRENDA'S PARENT'S HOUSE. - SUN PORCH - EVENING
Frank stands next to Roger in the library, the two men sipping brandy as they stare at a PAINTING OF PRESIDENT JOHNSON.

ROGER
It's just a hobby.

ROGER
Every Sunday night I go into the garage, pretend I'm Norman Rockwell. Sometimes I stay in there for hours, hiding from the world, making a fool out of myself.

Roger smiles, hands Frank a cigar.

ROGER
What about you, Frank? Where do you go when you need to hide?

FRANK
I just find Brenda. And then I don't need to hide.

ROGER
Did she tell you the truth about her pregnancy?

FRANK
Yes, Sir, she told me.

ROGER
Some people don't like to hear the truth. They're afraid of it. I'm not like that. So if you think my painting is bad, tell me now.

FRANK
No, Sir. You're an artist.

ROGER
And what are you? Because I think you're about to ask for my daughter's hand in marriage, and I have a right to know.

FRANK
Know what, Sir?

ROGER
The truth. Tell me the truth, Frank. What are you doing here? What is a man like you doing with Brenda?

FRANK
The truth?

ROGER
The truth, please. If you want my blessing, if you want my daughter, I'd like to hear it from you now.

Frank stares at Roger, watches as he sits on a red leather couch. There is a long BEAT as Frank slowly sits across from him, his hands shaking as he sets his drink down.

FRANK
The truth, Sir. The truth is...I'm not a Doctor. I'm not a lawyer. I'm not an airline pilot. I'm nothing, really. I'm just a kid who's in love with your daughter.

Roger sits up, keeps his eyes on Frank as he grabs his cigar and lights it.

ROGER
No. You know what you are? You're a romantic.

Frank has no idea what he's talking about.

ROGER
Men like us are nothing without the women we love. I have to admit, I'm guilty of the same foolish whimsy. I proposed to Carol after five dates with two nickels to my name and holes in my shoes — because I knew she was the one. So go ahead, Frank, ask the question you came here to ask me. Don't be afraid.

The Right Uniform

The movie takes place at a very seminal moment in our cultural history — those years between JFK and the cultural revolution. Frank Abagnale knew how to take advantage of the way we used to worship at the shrine of Saville Row and the Pan Am pilot; when how you dressed went a long way in determining who you were. The right uniform opened the world for Frank. Then the counterculture began to question those icons, but the movie captures that time when things were just beginning to change.

—WALTER F. PARKES AND LAURIE MACDONALD, PRODUCERS

FRANK
Sir, what would I have to do to take the bar here in New Orleans?

INT. - STATE BAR EXAMINERS OFFICE. - NEW ORLEANS. - DAY
CLOSE ON: BERKELEY TRANSCRIPTS, complete with Berkeley Logo and stationary. Frank hands the documents to a WOMAN sitting behind a desk, who hands him the LOUISIANA BAR EXAM.

BAR EXAMINER
Good luck, Mister Conners.

INT. - TWA PLANE. - DAY
SUPER: DECEMBER 26, 1969. TWA FLIGHT 676.

Carl Hanratty is sitting next to a handcuffed Frank at the back of the plane. Frank watches as Carl tries to peel the label off a tiny bottle of vodka. Amdursky and Fox are sitting across from them.

HANRATTY
Look at that. They show movies on planes now. What's next?

Frank and Carl stare at a small MOVIE SCREEN thirty rows in front of them.

FRANK
Are you gonna eat that éclair?

HANRATTY
Yeah. I'm gonna eat it later.

FRANK
Do you want to split it?

HANRATTY
No.

Propmaster

The amount of detail on any set is amazing. If an actor is holding a piece of paper in a scene, that piece of paper will always pertain to the story. A letter will have period stamps and a facsimile cancellation mark. I always give each actor a wallet with a driver's license from the state he's in and made out in the character's name. It helps him get into character.

We probably created between 100 and 150 documents for this movie, using all different grades of paper, for everything from checks, insurance forms, licenses, and FBI badges to birth certificates. But the most difficult were the items we needed when Leo was a lawyer. We had to create the Harvard graduation certificate, all the IDs, the resumes, and brochures. There was so much stuff! In one of my first meetings with Steven Spielberg, he was very, very clear that this all has to be perfect because he was really going to use the documents to tell the story.

—STEVE MELTON, PROPMASTER

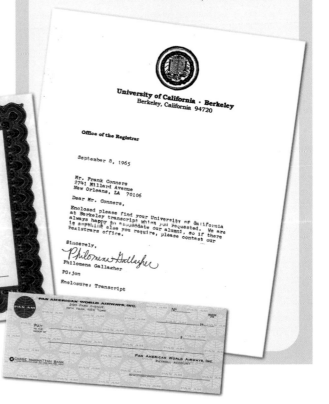

Carl moves his éclair away from Frank.

HANRATTY
You know what I could never figure out, Frank? How you cheated on the bar exam in Louisiana.

FRANK
What's the difference?

HANRATTY
Did you have somebody else take the test for you?

FRANK
I'm going to prison for a long time, Carl? What's the difference?

HANRATTY
You're right. It's a simple question.

FRANK
Give me half of the éclair and I'll tell you.

Carl carefully pulls the vodka label — but it rips in half.

HANRATTY
I'll figure it out eventually.

INT. - LOUISIANA DISTRICT ATTORNEY'S OFFICE. - DAY
Frank wears a new TAN SUIT and holds a TAN BRIEFCASE as he walks through the busy law office with Brenda's father.

ROGER
You'll be working under Phillip Rigby in corporate law, handling small claims made against the state, trespass-to-try-title suits.

Frank looks down at his desk, picks up the nameplate which reads: FRANK CONNERS, ASSISTANT PROSECUTOR.

ROGER
Why don't you settle in, organize your desk. We're having lunch with the District Attorney and Governor McKeithen at 12:30.

INT. - BRENDA'S PARENTS HOUSE. - NIGHT
Frank, Brenda, Roger, and Carol are eating popcorn and watching an episode of PERRY MASON on a black and white TV.

RAYMOND BURR (ON TV)
Look at this photograph, Mr. Stewart. It's a photograph of Prentice York, where they found him dead. Now here is an enlargement of that photograph — do you notice anything unusual about his shoe?

MR. STEWART
No. Nothing unusual.

RAYMOND BURR
It's unscuffed. It's unscuffed because you carried a dead man two miles to establish the lie that somehow Prentice York survived his brother! Why? Why?

INT. - NEW ORLEANS COURTROOM. - DAY
Frank stands in a small, empty courtroom, presenting a case before a JUDGE AT A PRE-TRIAL HEARING.

FRANK
This is a photograph of the defendant's signature taken from a cancelled check. Here is an enlargement of that signature, which matches the signature on the letters he wrote to Ms. Simon which discuss the possibility of defrauding the great state of Louisiana. Your honor, ladies and gentleman of the jury, this is irrefutable evidence that the defendant is lying!

JUDGE
Mister Conners, this is a preliminary hearing. There's no defendant, no jury, it's just me. What the hell is wrong with you?

EXT. - COURTROOM. - DAY
Frank walks out of the courtroom, where Roger is waiting for him.

ROGER
Well?

Frank starts to smile.

FRANK
They'll plead guilty and take three years in jail! I got the son of a bitch!

Frank shakes Roger's hand, and Roger pulls him close and gives him a hug.

INT. - CHURCH BINGO PARLOR. - DAY
Frank is sitting with Brenda and her family playing bingo in the packed church bingo hall.

BINGO CALLER
B-9. B-9.

FRANK
Bingo! I got it! Bingo! I got bingo again!

As Frank stands up, Carol and Roger are beaming with excitement.

CAROL
Two in one night! We got ourselves a good luck charm!

INT. - ROGER'S SUN PORCH. - DAY

Roger is painting a portrait of GEORGE WASHINGTON, copying it from a book. Frank is standing next to him at his own easel, carefully painting the same image. Frank's portrait is almost perfect, an exact copy of the original.

INT. - BRENDA'S PARENTS HOUSE. - NIGHT

Frank and Brenda are sitting alone on the couch watching the "SING ALONG WITH MITCH" SHOW ON TV.

Frank looks into the kitchen, watches as Roger and Carol wash the dishes together. They are talking and laughing quietly as they stand at the sink, their shoulders touching, a nightly ritual that resembles an intimate dance.

> **FRANK**
> Brenda...I love you.

Brenda turns to Frank, holds him tight.

> **BRENDA**
> Every time you say that I start to cry.

INT. - BRENDA'S ROOM. - NIGHT

Brenda's parents are tucking her in for the night. She's lying in a pink bed with a giant pink GIRAFFE next to her.

> **ROGER**
> Good night, sweetie.

They close Brenda's door, walk down the hall, and look in on Frank, who is wearing pajamas and lying on top of a small bed in the spare room. For the moment, he looks like a kid again.

> **CAROL**
> Frank, is there anything you need?

> **FRANK**
> Maybe I should go back to the hotel.

Roger and Carol walk into the room, stand over the bed.

> **ROGER**
> In a few months, you're gonna be part of this family. You're gonna be our son. You're not going to any hotel.

> **CAROL**
> Sleep tight, young man. I'm making peach-berry buckle in the morning.

EXT. - NEW ORLEANS GARDEN DISTRICT. - DAY

Frank is covering Brenda's eyes with his hands as he slowly walks her toward the front door of a LARGE HOUSE.

> **BRENDA**
> Hold me. Don't let me fall.

> **FRANK**
> Okay. We're here. Take a look.

Frank takes his hands away from her eyes, and Brenda stares up at a giant, six bedroom house that sits on a cul-de-sac. The house has a white picket fence, and looks a lot like Brenda's parents' house.

> **BRENDA**
> Frank, what is this?

> **FRANK**
> Look upstairs.

Brenda looks up at the house, sees the HUGE PINK GIRAFFE — the head sticking out of the second story window with a red bow tied around its neck.

> **BRENDA**
> What's Mr. Long Johns doing here?

> **FRANK**
> This is his new home, Brenda. It's our new home. We'll move in right after the wedding.

> **BRENDA**
> Oh, God. Oh, my God...

Brenda screams as she throws herself at Frank.

> **BRENDA**
> It's so big. Where will we get the money to buy a house like this?

> **FRANK**
> The same place everyone gets it.

Brenda holds onto Frank, her body shaking as he whispers in her ear. A TAXI pulls up and parks in the driveway.

> **FRANK**
> I have to go away for a few days, but I'll be back on Monday. I don't want you to be scared, Brenda, this will be the last time I ever leave you.

BRENDA
Where are you going?

FRANK
I'm going to get my parents.

BRENDA
On Christmas? You can't, Frank, we're supposed to go caroling after church?

FRANK
I promise, Brenda. This is the last time I'll ever leave you.

As Frank walks toward the CAB, WE SEE his hand reach into his pocket, slowly pull out the PAN AM GOLD STRIPES, which he places on his jacket.

INT. - WHITE CADILLAC - NIGHT
CLOSE ON: BRENDA CRYING.

Rain is pouring over a WHITE CADILLAC that is parked in front of a NEW ORLEANS AIRPORT TERMINAL. Brenda is in the passenger seat, clutching the key to the new house as she tries to compose herself.

FRANK
Brenda, look at me. I'm only gonna be gone for a few days.

BRENDA
Why can't I go with you? I want to meet your parents. I've never been on an airplane before.

FRANK
You need to stay here, help your Mother with the party.

BRENDA
But tomorrow is Christmas Eve. We always go caroling after church.

FRANK
I just need to go home for a few days, Brenda. And then I'll never leave you again.

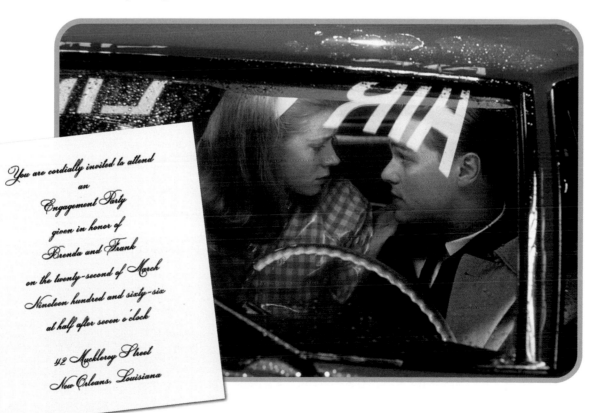

Frank's anchor is his father. He keeps coming back to the old man in New York. He keeps trying to win his approval and do all the things that the old man could not do. I think he wants his father to live vicariously through him, but it never works. By the end of his journey, he realizes he has to walk alone and so does his father. We cannot live through or for each other. We have to live for ourselves.

—Martin Sheen

INT. - BAR. - EASTCHESTER. - DAY
Frank walks into the bar wearing his black suit and holding the lawyer's briefcase. He sees his father sitting in the corner wearing a POSTMAN'S UNIFORM and drinking a beer.

The place is is filled with the scattered afternoon regulars, all drinking and watching TV. Frank walks up to his Dad and motions to the waitress.

> **FRANK**
> A Coca-Cola please.

Frank Sr. looks up, stares at his son.

> **FRANK SR.**
> Sit down, Frank. I'm so glad to see you.

> **FRANK**
> Dad...why are you dressed like that?

> **FRANK SR.**
> I took a job. A government job. You see what I'm doing? Do you have a good lawyer?

> **FRANK**
> Dad... I am a lawyer.

> **FRANK SR.**
> Look at this letter.
> (*handing him the letter*)
> The IRS wants more. I had a deal with them — two penalties — they ate the cake and now they want the crumbs. They think they can scare me, intimidate me — I'll make them chase me for the rest of my life.

> **FRANK**
> Dad...I came to give you this. It's an invitation to an engagement party.

Frank hands his father the invitation.

> **FRANK**
> I'm getting married, Dad. You don't have to worry.

> **FRANK**
> I'm buying a $60,000 house — a new Cadillac — everything they took from us, I'm getting it back.

Frank suddenly stops, his smile fading as he looks at his father for a long BEAT — sees the name ABAGNALE stitched on the patch of the blue jacket.

> **FRANK**
> Has Mom seen you dressed like that?

> **FRANK SR.**
> I'm beating them at their own game, Frank. I'm one of them now — a government employee — you see how beautiful that is?

> **FRANK**
> You can't let her see you.

> **FRANK SR.**
> She came to pick up some boxes at the apartment.

> **FRANK**
> We have to go see her right now. We'll tell her about the wedding, you can ask her to come...

FRANK SR.
She won't see me, Frank.

FRANK
Then you have to call her, tell her you're not a postman. Tell her it was a mistake.

Frank takes a dime out of his pocket.

FRANK
Here. Just call her. Take the money and call her. I bought you plane tickets... you'll come together.

FRANK SR.
She's married now. She married my friend, Jack Barnes. They have a house in Long Island.

Frank is clearly upset as the WAITRESS brings over a shot for his father. Frank Sr. reaches out and slowly pulls it in.

FRANK SR.
You've really got their number, Frank. I had an FBI Agent in my apartment, he looked scared.

FRANK
Dad...it's over. I'm gonna stop.

FRANK SR.
The United States government, Frank, running for the hills.

FRANK
I'll talk to Mom. We'll go and get you a suit. A new black suit. One of those Manhattan Eagle three button black pearls.

FRANK SR.
They're never gonna catch you, Frank. Why won't you sit down?

Frank looks around the bar.

FRANK SR.
Come on, sit with me and have a drink. I'm your father.

FRANK
Then why don't you ask me to stop?

Frank Sr. stares up at his son, then slowly sits back and sips his drink.

FRANK
Why don't you ask me, Dad? Why don't you tell me?

FRANK SR.
Because you can't stop.

Frank looks scared as he watches his father drink. He slowly backs up, knocks over a few chairs.

FRANK SR.
Come on, Frank — don't go. Where are you going?

Frank never looks back as he turns to run out of the bar.

FRANK SR.
Where you going tonight? Tahiti? Hawaii? Where you going?

Frank Sr. slowly reaches out, puts his palm over a single DIME that is sitting in front of him on the table.

Prudence was a quality I did not seem to possess.

I was actually incapable of sound judgment, I realize now, driven by compulsions over which I had no control. I was now living by rationalizations: I was the hunted, the police were the hunters, ergo, the police were the bad guys. I had to steal to survive, to finance my continual flight from the bad guys, consequently, I was justified in my illegal means of support.... I was fully aware that I was on a mad carrousel ride, a merry-go-round whirling ungoverned from which I seemed unable to dismount, but I sure as hell didn't want cops to stop the whirligig.
—Frank W. Abagnale, from his book

INT. - CARL HANRATTY'S OFFICE. - NIGHT

Carl is waiting in his office with Fox and Amdursky, who look bored as they eat Chinese food from cartons. The phone rings, and Carl quickly answers.

> **HANRATTY**
> This is Hanratty.

> **FRANK**
> Hello, Carl. Merry Christmas.

Carl grabs a pad and pencil as Fox and Amdursky listen in on their own phones.

> **HANRATTY**
> What do you want, Doctor Conners?

> **FRANK**
> Carl, I haven't been Doctor Conners for months now.

> **HANRATTY**
> Shut up. I'm sitting here in my office on Christmas Eve, so just tell me what you want.

> **FRANK**
> It's over. I want it to be over now. I'm getting married. I'm settling down.

> **HANRATTY**
> You've stolen almost $4 million. You think we're just gonna call it a wedding present? This isn't something you get to walk away from, Frank.

> **FRANK**
> I want to call a truce.

> **HANRATTY**
> There is no truce. You will be caught, and you will go to prison. Where did you think this was going?

> **FRANK**
> Please, leave me alone, Carl. I don't want to do it anymore. Don't make me do it anymore.

> **HANRATTY**
> I'm close, aren't I? You're scared because I'm getting close. I know you rented that car in Shreveport, you stayed in that hotel on Lake Charles. You want to run, be my guest — because the checks don't lie as well as you do.

> **FRANK**
> Will you stop chasing me?

> **HANRATTY**
> I can't stop. Ever. It's my job.

> **FRANK**
> It's okay, Carl. I just thought I'd ask.

The line goes dead, and Carl turns to Fox and Amdursky.

> **HANRATTY**
> Get every newspaper you can find. Every newspaper in Louisiana for the last two months.

> **FOX**
> What are we looking for?

> **HANRATTY**
> Engagement announcements. Last name Conners.

> **AMDURSKY**
> Conners? Come on, Carl, he would have changed it by now.

HANRATTY
He can't change it. She thinks he's Conners. If he loses the name, he loses the girl.

INT. - AIRPLANE. - COCKPIT. - NIGHT
Frank is hidden in the shadows of the cockpit, strapped into the JUMP SEAT, his face coming in and out of the light as he looks out the window — the skyline of New York City fading in the distance. The PILOT gets out of his seat, turns back to Frank.

PILOT
We're leveled off. You mind taking her for a minute? I need to use the bathroom.

The Pilot walks out of the cockpit, and Frank looks a bit confused. After a long BEAT he slowly gets out of the JUMP-SEAT, walks over and sits in the PILOT'S SEAT, sees that the AUTO-PILOT light is on.

He stares at the blackness in front of him — his hands starting to shake as he slowly reaches out and puts them on the wheel — tears starting to flow as he flies the plane into the night.

ROGER (V.O.)
Ladies and gentleman, may I have your attention, please. It is time to bring out the guests of honor.

INT. - BRENDA'S PARENTS' HOUSE. - DOWNSTAIRS. - AFTERNOON
A party is in progress. BRENDA'S FATHER is surrounded by a sea of
guests, all of whom are drinking and laughing and dancing to a three-
piece dixieland band. WAITERS push their way through the party as
the festive crowd fills every corner of the massive house.

The band stops playing as Carol brings Roger a fresh drink.

> **ROGER**
> I'm not a man who normally believes in luck or gypsy fortune — so
> standing here tonight I am convinced that divine fate has blessed
> this house, and that this union is a work of art that has been paint-
> ed by the grand master himself. Ladies and gentlemen — raise your
> glasses to my baby girl, Brenda May, and her fiancée — my future
> son-in-law — Doctor Frank Allen Conners Esquire.

CLOSE ON: FRANK AND BRENDA, standing arm-in-arm at the top
of the stairs, both looking a bit overwhelmed as the guests start
applauding, the cheers rising as they slowly descend.

Frank wears a blue pin-striped suit, and Brenda a pink lace dress.

INT. - PARTY. - LATER THAT NIGHT
Guests have separated Frank and Brenda, the men surrounding Frank —
the women forming a circle around Brenda, who is showing off her ring.

> **FRANK**
> Excuse me.

Frank makes his way through the party, smiling at guests, staring at
the servants, the food — the EXPENSIVE suits that have filled the
room. He walks up the stairs, stands in the shadows as he hides from
the world that he is about to enter.

And then it hits him — BRIGHT LIGHTS knifing through the windows
OF THE HOUSE — HEADLIGHTS finding Frank in the dark and filling the upstairs for a few seconds — then throwing it all back into
darkness.

Frank stands frozen for a BEAT, then carefully moves along the landing
as he looks toward the front door of the house — sees one of the
MAIDS answering the door.

She's keeping the door half closed, nervously looking around as she
talks to a MAN in a brown coat with brown shoes. As Frank stands at
the railing, he sees CARL HANRATTY standing on the porch, holding
up his wallet and showing off his badge.

A HAND taps Frank on the shoulder, and he quickly turns and faces
Brenda, unable to hide the fear in
his eyes. Brenda is smiling and
holding a stack of envelopes.

> **BRENDA**
> Frank, I've been looking for
> you. Can you hold all these
> checks?

Frank takes Brenda by the hand,
pulls her back from the landing —

CLOSE ON: CARL HANRATTY —
standing on the porch as Roger
Strong walks toward him.

> **HANRATTY**
> Carl Hanratty, FBI. Sorry to
> crash your party, Sir.

ROGER
What can I do for you?

HANRATTY
Well, if it wouldn't be too much trouble. I'd like to meet the groom.

INT. - FRANK'S BEDROOM. - NIGHT
Frank rushes into the bedroom, moves toward the windows and looks out on the front of the house. Lanterns line the driveway and twinkle lights hang from the trees as he stares down at Hanratty's car, which is parked in the driveway. Frank rushes toward the closet, pulls out two suitcases.

BRENDA
Frank, what's wrong?

FRANK
We have to leave, Brenda.

Frank opens the suitcases, which are stuffed with money. He shoves some of his clothes on top of the money, trying to make it fit.

FRANK
You love me, right? I mean, you would love me no matter what?

BRENDA
What's wrong? Don't you like the party?

FRANK
If I was poor, or sick, or if I had a different name.

BRENDA
Where did you get all that money?

FRANK
A name means nothing, right? My name is Frank Conners. That's who I am with you. We all have secrets. Sometimes when I travel, I use the name Frank Taylor. That's my secret.

BRENDA
Frank Taylor?

FRANK
It means nothing — Frank Taylor, Frank Black — when I'm with you, I'm Frank Conners — that's all that matters.

Frank takes some of the money out, shoves it under the bed so he can get the rest of his clothes inside.

BRENDA
Why are you saying all this?

FRANK
Brenda, I don't want to lie anymore. I'm not a doctor. I never went to medical school.

Brenda studies him, trying to understand.

FRANK
And I'm not a lawyer or a Harvard graduate or a Lutheran. I ran away from home a year and a half ago when I was sixteen.

To this day, I don't drink, I don't smoke, and I've never used drugs. But I was always addicted to women, even at a very young age. I like women. I like being with them and I really never had any apology for having met all the women I could when I was young. I never took any of those relationships seriously because I was only a kid and the women were always older. There was no way I was going to get married then and, even if I wanted to, I wasn't legally old enough. I always treated the relationships casually.

If I thought a girl was getting serious, I ended the relationship. In the film, the character of Brenda represents an actual girl I did meet and that was the one relationship that did get serious. Consequently, I felt the need to be honest with her and tell her who I was and what I did. And, in the movie and in real life, she betrayed me — or I should say, what I believed was betrayal at that age and at that time. Now, of course, I realize she did the right thing by turning me in, but I didn't see it that way at that time. Back then it only reinforced my feeling that I couldn't trust people. After Brenda, I never revealed my true identity to anyone.

—Frank W. Abagnale, on the movie

116

BRENDA
Frank...you're not a Lutheran?

FRANK
See all this money — I have more —
I have lots more. Enough for the rest
of our lives.

BRENDA
Stop teasing me, Frank. You're Frank
Conners, right? You're Frank Conners,
and you're 28 years old. Why would
you lie to me?

Brenda turns to Frank, trying not to get
upset.

BRENDA
Frank, what's your name? I want you to
tell me your name.

FRANK
We'll go to Liverpool. We can live there,
Brenda, you and I can live wherever we
want. But you're gonna have to trust me.
Do you trust me? Do you love me?

BRENDA
I love you.

Frank throws open the window — lifts the
cases to the ledge.

FRANK
No matter what. Even if we have to live
in Liverpool, or I have a different name
— you'll still love me?

BRENDA
(*upset*)
I love you, Frank. I love you. I just want
to be with you.

FRANK
In two days you're gonna meet me at
Miami International Airport. You'll leave
the house after your parents go to sleep,
you'll take a taxi and give him this
money — tell him to drive through the
night. I'll meet you there at ten o'clock.

Frank hands her a stack of $100 bills.

BRENDA
But the wedding is next month. It's all planned. We can leave right
after the reception, just like a honeymoon.

FRANK
No, Brenda, you have to listen to me. The international terminal in
Miami, there's an Eastern Airlines flight to London. Say it, Brenda,
no matter what! You'll take a taxi — say you'll be there at ten o'clock!

BRENDA
Ten o'clock. No matter what.

Frank steps toward her, holds her in his arms.

FRANK
Two days. We'll get married in Liverpool. And we'll never tell anyone, Brenda. Promise me you'll never tell anyone?

As Carl

Hanratty, I'm as perennial as the sun. I never change.

Of course, the real Carl Hanratty is not named Carl Hanratty, though the character is based on an FBI agent who did track Frank Abagnale. Hanratty specialized in working bank fraud and took great pride in his job.

One day he discovers this paper-hanger, as they're called, who is doing magnificently smart, intelligent work, several notches above the average check forger. Carl makes it his life mission to track him down and catch him, if he can.

Although Carl is impressed with the style, the panache, and the success ratio of Abagnale, he's doubly astound-ed to discover that this paperhanger is just a kid—an incredibly talented kid—but still, he's a child who is in the midst of an adventure larger than his own experience. Carl comes to feel almost protective of this young man. He treats him as a criminal, he's going to arrest him, he's going to put him in jail, but, at the end of the day, he also worries about the boy's soul.

I think Carl sees Frank as a kin-dred spirit; perhaps as the son Carl never had. So Carl goes from treating him as this punk crook to thinking of him as a fragile human being worth trying to redeem.

—Tom Hanks

BRENDA
I promise. I love you, Frank. I'll always love you. But please, before you go — tell me your name.

INT. - PARTY. - MOMENTS LATER
Hanratty is moving through the crowd, taking in the incredible scenery of this world — smiling at some of the guests as he awkwardly tries to follow Roger Strong through the room.

ROGER
Has anyone seen our bride and groom?

Carl stops walking — something next to the bar has caught his eye. He sees two bottles of CHAMPAGNE chilling on ice. As he moves toward the bottles, he SEES that their labels have been PEELED AWAY, TORN RIGHT DOWN THE MIDDLE.

CAROL
I think they went upstairs.

ON HANRATTY: moving quickly now, making his way up the stairs — his left hand in his jacket calmly searching for his gun as he finds himself on the upstairs landing, moving from room to room —

Carl opens several doors, and finally stops at the end of the hall. He throws open the door to Brenda's room, sees her sitting on the edge of the bed crying, several $100 BILLS blowing around the floor as a breeze pushes in from the open window.

INT. - BRENDA'S PARENTS HOUSE. -NIGHT.
The house is empty — the party over. Roger and Carol are sitting in the library with Brenda, holding her in their arms as two POLICE OFFICERS stand across from them. Brenda is crying, her stuffed giraffe lying next to her, a small white CAT in her lap. Carl Hanratty walks into the room with Amdursky and Fox.

I **was** shooting my first (and only) scene with Tom Hanks, and Steven Spielberg was standing right outside the doorway. I hear him go, "Hey, Amy!"

"Yeah, Steven?"

He says, "You're acting with Tom Hanks!"

And I thought, "Yes, I am, oh my gosh, I am!"

—Amy Adams

HANRATTY
Hello, Brenda. You feeling better now?

Brenda just stares at him.

HANRATTY
Do you remember my name? It's Carl.

ROGER
Go ahead, Brenda. Talk to this man. Tell him what you know.

HANRATTY
Would it be okay if I spoke to her alone?

Brenda keeps her face buried in her father's shirt, tries to hold onto him. Roger gives her a kiss, takes Carol out of the room.

HANRATTY
That's a pretty cat. What's his name?

BRENDA
Ringo.

HANRATTY
I know this is all a bit scary, Brenda, but I need you to tell me where Frank is going. A lot of people are looking for him out there, and the last thing we want is for Frank to get hurt. And I swear to you, Brenda, if you tell me where he's going — I'll try to keep him safe.

BRENDA
I can't tell you.

HANRATTY
Because you made a promise? Is that right, Brenda? You made a promise?

Brenda slowly nods.

HANRATTY
Then forget it. I won't ask you again. A promise is a promise.

Hanratty sits on the couch next to her. He reaches out and picks up the pink giraffe.

HANRATTY
My little girl used to have a giraffe like this. What's his name?

EXT. MIAMI INTERNATIONAL AIRPORT. - MORNING
The outside of the airport is jammed, cars and people scrambling toward the terminal buildings. Police Officers direct traffic as lines of TAXIS wait for the morning flights to arrive.

CLOSE ON FRANK
Sitting in the front seat of a rental car, looking down at his gold watch, which reads 10:00 A.M.

Frank is waiting in the main parking lot, which sits directly across from the international terminal, his nondescript car surrounded by hundreds more.

The Color Arc of the Movie

We talked for a long time about the color arc of emotion in the movie. We decided that Frank would start in a kind of ordinary beige, a normal but not terribly colorful, slightly monochromatic, environment. As he got better and better at his game, the colors would get wilder and wilder. It was convenient for us that he also moves from the North to the South while this change is happening. In the South, we were able to play with oranges, yellows, reds, and pinks — vibrant, wilder colors and tones. Then, when he has to flee the United States, he's back in an unknown territory so the scenes in France are not terribly colorful. At the end of the film, he's blending into the relatively mono-chromatic bureaucracy of grays, blues, and browns. Here there is more black and white because his life is clearer and more boring once he's settled down. In the end, he's come back to where he's started in terms of color. I think it's fascinating to watch the character move through the color of the sets.

—JEANNINE OPPEWALL,
PRODUCTION DESIGNER

These two photographs of Leonardo DiCaprio demonstrate the color arc of the movie as the clothes and sets move from muted, monochromatic colors to wilder and more vibrant colors.

He watches as a TAXI pulls up to the international terminal — a smile coming over his face as he sees Brenda getting out of the cab and paying the driver. She holds a pink suitcase, and looks a bit lost as she stands in front of the terminal for a BEAT.

Frank gets out of his car, is about to move toward her — when something catches his eye. He looks toward the CAB that Brenda was in, sees that the driver hasn't gotten in the cab line. He's still parked in front of the terminal —

Frank looks toward the TRAFFIC COPS — sees that they have one eye on the road — one eye on Brenda —

Frank sees a LIMO parked in front of the terminal — A VAN is circling — TWO REPAIR MEN are fixing an antenna on the roof — BRENDA ISN'T MOVING. She's standing in front of the terminal, waiting for something — looking out at the cars and the people — then almost imperceptibly — her eyes glance toward the VAN —

Frank falls back into his car — his mind racing as he watches the scene unfold, the anger slowly starting to rise inside of him as Brenda disappears into the terminal.

INT. TEMPORARY OFFICE. - MIAMI AIRPORT. - DAY
Carl Hanratty stands in front of 20 FBI AGENTS, pacing.

> **HANRATTY**
> We have to stop him before he leaves the country.

> **FOX**
> He doesn't have a passport.

> **HANRATTY**
> In the last six months, he's gone to Harvard and Berkeley — I'm betting he can get a passport. I want everyone we have inside Miami International. He's used it before, he knows the layout.

> **AMDURSKY**
> I already talked to the Miami police, they've offered 50 uniformed cops in 2 shifts of 25.

> **FOX**
> Carl, with our guys that's almost a hundred men in one airport. Don't you think we should spread it around?

> **HANRATTY**
> No. This will be the exit point.

> **AMDURSKY**
> How do you know he won't go to New York, Atlanta?

> **HANRATTY**
> Because I'm not in Atlanta.

EXT. - MIAMI HOTEL PAY PHONE. - DAY
Frank is inspecting a phony PASSPORT as he talks on the hotel pay phone, a perfect Miami sunset behind him.

> **FRANK (ON PHONE)**
> This is Frank Roberts, and I'm letting all the universities in the area know that Pan Am will be initiating a new recruiting program this year. I'll be stopping by your campus tomorrow morning.

INT. - NORTH MIAMI COLLEGE. - AUDITORIUM. - DAY
Three hundred students, ALL FEMALE, staring up at MR. HENDRICKS, the DIRECTOR OF STUDENT PLACEMENT.

> **MR. HENDRICKS**
> Ladies, quiet down, please. As you all know, Pan Am has sent a pilot here to interview prospective stewardesses for a new internship program. You have to be at least 21 years old with a valid passport. This is Captain Roberts, and he'll be talking to you today.

Frank stands in front of the girls, who suddenly get very quiet.

FRANK
Thank you all for coming. At the end of the day I'll be picking eight young ladies to be part of Pan Am's first "future stewardess" flight crew program. These eight girls will accompany me on a two month public relations tour of Europe, where they will learn firsthand what it takes to be a Pan Am stewardess.

EXT. - MIAMI INTERNATIONAL AIRPORT. - DAY
WE SEE FBI AGENTS, UNIFORMED COPS, UNDERCOVER COPS, and local detectives all taking their positions in and around the airport. It looks like they're preparing for war, and Carl Hanratty is in the middle of it all.

INT. - INTERVIEW ROOM. - NORTH MIAMI COLLEGE. - DAY
Frank sits behind a desk holding a notebook as he INTERVIEWS a young FEMALE STUDENT.

FRANK
Judy, how many emergency exits are there on a 707?

JUDY
Four? Six?

INT. - INTERVIEW ROOM. - LATER
Frank has drawn a picture of an AIRPLANE ON A CHALKBOARD. He is pointing to various sections of the plane.

FRANK
And what's this, Monica?

MONICA
Forward lav.

FRANK
Very good. And this?

MONICA
Aft lav.

FRANK
Excellent.

INT. - INTERVIEW ROOM. - LATER. - MONTAGE
Frank interviewing VARIOUS FEMALE STUDENTS.

ON MIGGY

MIGGY
On the right side of the plane you'll see Mount Rainer — the highest peak in the state of California.

FRANK
Washington.

MIGGY
Washington. Shoot.

ON KAREN

KAREN
If I were elected to be one of the future stewardesses, I'd do my very best to represent Pan Am, to represent my home state of Florida and all the needy children throughout the United States of America.

ON IRIS

IRIS
Can I get you a pillow, Sir? A blanket? A copy of *Life* magazine?

ON ILENE

ILENE
As you can see, there are two exits at the front of the plane, and two in the back.

FRANK
Rear.

ILENE
Rear. Right. Sorry. Can I try it again?

ON CANDY

CANDY
We'll be traveling at 6,000 miles per hour with an altitude of 300 feet.

ON MIGGY

MIGGY
I think I should be chosen as a future stewardess because I'm friendly, caring, and I've always wanted to see the continent of Europe.

ON FRANK

FRANK
Okay. I'd like you all to take out your books, put them on your heads. Let's see how well you can walk.

ON IRIS

IRIS
Forward lav. After lav. Backward lav.

Stewardess Chic

Ut was great fun to research the uniforms for the pilots and stewardesses. Very memorable to me was this industrial film that Pan Am Airlines had produced in the early 1960s called *Come Fly With Me*. It introduces a young woman who has just been hired by Pan Am and follows the step-by-step transformation into the perfect Pan Am stewardess. Eyebrows are shaped, hair is groomed, etiquette is taught, posture is perfected, and the uniform is fitted. I could pause the frame and examine the construction, cut, and details of the uniform that were so specific to that time period.

In the 1960s, getting a job as a stewardess was a very big deal. The job and the lifestyle were very glamorous. In those days, air travel was the domain of the well-to-do, passengers traveled in their Sunday best and stewardesses had to be up to par. There were also a fair amount of matrimonial unions between stewardesses and the eligible passengers.

I tried very hard to be historically accurate with all of the stewardess uniforms, but I took some liberties with color selection for storytelling purposes. The Pan Am uniform changed in 1965, so I introduced the new uniforms on the eight coeds that Frank uses as a decoy at the Miami airport. I used a brighter blue here so the girls made a greater impact visually.

—MARY ZOPHRES,
COSTUME DESIGNER

FRANK
Forward. Aft. Rear. Try again.

ON DAPHNE

DAPHNE
(*pointing to a plane*)
Wing, tail, nose...

ON PEGGY

PEGGY
I was fourth runner-up at the junior Miss Miami pageant last year.

ON STARR

STARR
My mother is a housewife and my father is a police officer.

FRANK
Your Dad's a cop? Perfect.

INT. - AUDITORIUM - DAY
This is the moment of truth. All the girls are standing, and Frank is reading from a list.

FRANK
Debra Jo McMillian.

DEBRA JO comes screaming out from the sea of girls, hugging friends and crying as if she had just won the Ms. America Pageant.

FRANK
Heather Shack.

HEATHER SHACK screams and rushes into Debra Jo's arms, the two girls screaming as Frank continues to announce the winners.

The images on these pages are part of the phony publicity tour Frank arranged in Europe with his own air crew.

My fantasies of an aircrew of my own, of course, were motivated by more than just a desire for companionship. An aircrew — and I thought of an aircrew only in terms of stewardesses — would lend concrete validity to my role of an airline pilot. I had learned that a solitary pilot was always subject to scrutiny. Conversely, a pilot trailing a squad of lovely stewardesses would almost certainly be above suspicion. If I had a beautiful bevy of flight attendants with me in my travels, I could scatter my valueless checks like confetti, and they'd be accepted like rice at a wedding, I thought. Not that I was having any trouble passing them at present, but I was passing them one at a time. With a crew behind me, I could cash the sham checks in multiple numbers. . . .Mine was a plan that demanded the boldness of a mountain climber. . . .Riding herd on eight lovely, vivacious, exuberant, energetic girls is akin to a cowboy riding herd on a bunch of wild steers while mounted on a lame horse —- damned near impossible. I had determined at the outset of the scheme that there would be no personal involvement with any of the girls, but my resolve was endangered a score of times during the course of the summer. Each of them was an outrageous flirt, and I, of course, was a prince of philanderers, and when one of the girls was inclined to make a sexual advance (and each of them did on several occasions), I was hardly prone to fend her off. But I always managed.

—Frank W. Abagnale, from his book

EXT. - MIAMI INTERNATIONAL AIRPORT. - DAY
Miami Police Officers are spread out in front of the airport,
looking bored as they drink coffee and pace back and forth.

A STATION WAGON pulls up to the front of the airport, and TWO
COPS WATCH as EIGHT BEAUTIFUL COLLEGE GIRLS walk out, all
dressed as flight attendants, all holding luggage.

The cops never even glance at Frank, who stands in the middle of the
girls as they walk into the airport.

INT. - MIAMI INTERNATIONAL AIRPORT. - DAY
Frank walks through the packed terminal surrounded by the EIGHT
GIRLS, all walking in stride, their hair and make-up perfect, every
man in the airport turning to stare.

Frank and the girls walk past TWO FBI AGENTS, who can't help but
smile at the girls — who in turn smile back.

>   **FBI AGENT #1**
>   Did you see that blonde in front?

>   **FBI AGENT #2**
>   I should've been a pilot.

Carl Hanratty is standing on the second floor looking down over the
entire INTERNATIONAL TERMINAL. HE HEARS an announcement
over the airport P.A. system.

>   **P.A. OPERATOR (V.O.)**
>   Will Mr. Carl Hanratty pick up a white courtesy phone? Mr. Carl
>   Hanratty, please pick up a white courtesy phone.

In the distance, CARL watches as the eight girls walk toward him. He
hesitates for a BEAT, then walks to the back of the restaurant and finds
a WHITE PHONE.

>   **HANRATTY**
>   This is Hanratty.

>AMDURSKY
>
>Carl, you're walkie-talkie wasn't working. There's a guy in a Pan Am uniform sitting in a white Cadillac in front of Terminal J!

>HANRATTY
>
>That's the charter terminal. Can you see his face?

>AMDURSKY
>
>He's got his Pilot's cap on. I think it's him!

INT. - AIRPORT. - DAY

Carl Hanratty is running through the airport, sprinting past Frank and the college girls as he makes his way outside.

EXT. - WHITE CADILLAC. - DAY

FORTY FBI AGENTS and MIAMI POLICE OFFICERS slowly approach the white Cadillac. Carl Hanratty has his gun drawn.

>HANRATTY
>
>Frank, get out of the car! Put your hands on the hood! There's no place to run, so just make it easy on yourself!

The car door opens, and a 20-YEAR-OLD kid gets out of the car, his hands shaking as he stares at Carl — the pilot's cap falling off his head.

>KID
>
>Don't shoot me! I'm just a driver! A man paid me a hundred dollars to wear this uniform and pick someone up at the airport!

>HANRATTY
>
>Who are you picking up?

>KID
>
>Carl Hanratty.

Carl lowers his gun, immediately turns back toward the airport — watches as a BRITISH AIRWAYS JET takes off and flies overhead, banking left and sailing out over the ocean.

INT. - CARL HANRATTY'S OFFICE. - WASHINGTON, D.C. - DAY

Snow is falling outside Carl's office window, which overlooks a parking lot. Carl sits at his desk trying to peel a label off of a coffee can. As the label rips, a SECRETARY WALKS in and hands him an envelope.

>SECRETARY
>
>This just came for you, Sir. Who do you know in Liverpool?

Carl takes the envelope and slowly opens it. He pulls out a stack of BLACK AND WHITE PHOTOGRAPHS, all of which show the EIGHT COLLEGE GIRLS in various locations. There are shots of them on the SPANISH STEPS IN ROME, at the EIFFEL TOWER, in front of BUCK-INGHAM PALACE, and in front of SCOT-LAND YARD.

A PAN AM CHECK is inside the envelope, with the words "THE LAST ONE" written across the back.

EXT. - MONTRICHARD, FRANCE. - DAY

The vineyards of Montrichard stretch across the Loire Valley. Frank is eating an ice cream as he walks through town, the shops and restaurants open and busy for the summer. Frank stops a DELIVERY BOY on a bicycle.

>FRANK
>
>Excuse me. Do you know where the Lavalier family lives?

I had crisscrossed the globe from Singapore to Stockholm, from Tahiti to Trieste, from Baltimore to the Baltics, and to other places I had forgotten I'd visited.

But one place I had not forgotten. And its name kept popping into my thoughts as I sought a safe haven. Montpellier, France.

Montpellier. That was my safe haven, I finally decided. And having made the decision, I didn't give it a second thought.

I should have.

—Frank W. Abagnale, from his book
(In the movie, he goes to Montrichard, France.)

EXT. - LAVALIER HOME. - DAY
Frank is knocking on the door of small house. He hears screaming coming from the backyard, and he walks along the side of the house and finds OLIVER, 9, having a mud fight with his mother, MONIQUE, who is caked in dirt and laughing so hard she's crying. Two large dogs are barking and playing with them — and Monique is trying to hide behind an old swing set.

Oliver and Monique stop, turn to stare at Frank.

>   **FRANK**
>   My name is Frank. My mother is Paula Lavalier. I was hoping to find Patrice, her brother.

PATRICE walks out of the house, stares at Frank. His shirt is off, and he's drinking a beer.

>   **MONIQUE**
>   Patrice. This is your nephew.

Patrice slowly walks toward Frank, stares down at him for a LONG BEAT. Monique and Oliver stay back.

>   **PATRICE**
>   You are Paula's son?

>   **FRANK**
>   Yes.

>   **PATRICE**
>   What do you want?

ABOVE: The Place Royale in Quebec City, Canada filled in for Montrichard, France. An existing structure on the Place was painstakingly transformed with aged signage and building materials into the print shop — or Imprimerie (LEFT) — where Frank is ultimately arrested by Hanratty.

Frank escapes from the FBI in the most clever way. He perceives that he's being pursued and he goes off camera and invents a fabulous way of deceiving his pursuers. He walks out and evaporates into a crowd. He's like a decorator crab that walks along the bottom of the ocean looking for things to attach to himself in order to blend in with the local vegetation. In the same way, Frank is always taking things from his environment and cobbling them onto himself. He's sneaking right under the radar screen and the noses of the FBI.

—Jeannine Oppewall,
Production Designer

130

FRANK
To see you. To see my family.

Patrice stares at Frank, hands him the beer.

PATRICE
Okay, nephew. Come take a look.

INT. - LAVALIER HOME. - DINNER TABLE. - LATE
The family is sitting around the dinner table, quietly talking in French. Relatives from the village have filled the house — it's like a family reunion as everyone stares at Frank. Patrice sits at the head of the table silently watching.

PATRICE
Tell me about Paula. In her last letter she told me she was learning to play tennis.

FRANK
When was that?

PATRICE
Fifteen years ago.

Frank stares at Patrice, then turns to the family and smiles.

FRANK
Mom is the queen of Manhattan, famous for her parties — they're always in the newspaper.

As Oliver translates, the entire room stares at Frank.

FRANK
We live in the city, right on Park Avenue. Dad is a stockbroker on Wall Street. And I have a new baby sister. She just turned one.

MONIQUE
Her name?

FRANK
Her name is Brenda.

Frank takes a sip of wine, starts to gag. Everyone laughs as Frank reaches for his water.

PATRICE
You like the wine? Monique's family owns all the vineyards you see behind the house. The worst wine in France.

MONIQUE
Leave me alone.

FRANK
I think it's good.

Patrice starts to laugh again, and Monique looks upset as she gets up from the table.

PATRICE
He likes it. You hear that, Monique? My sister can sell it on Park Avenue!

INT. - LAVALIER HOME. - NIGHT
Frank is sitting in the living room staring down at a photo album. He sees the old picture of his mother and father sitting on the American tank. Monique hands him a faded black and white photograph.

OLIVER
Can Frank stay here with us while he goes to school?

> **Most of** the movie was shot on the West Coast. We moved to Montreal for three days and shot the French scenes there. We shot the French prison scenes in a Montreal prison. We also did three days in New York, shooting exteriors and bank interiors. We could not find those cathedral-like bank lobbies on the West Coast.
> —Walter F. Parkes and Laurie MacDonald, Producers

FRANK
I thought I might take a few classes at the university.

Before Monique can answer, Patrice walks into the room, and everyone stares up at him.

PATRICE
He can stay one week. Then he gets an apartment.

MONIQUE
Two weeks.

Oliver stares at his mother, surprised to hear her say this. Patrice is also surprised, and he can't help but smile.

PATRICE
Two weeks.

EXT. - MONTRICHARD VINEYARD. - DAY
Frank is chasing Oliver through the Vineyards, heading for an open field. Oliver is kicking a soccer ball, showing Frank how to do it, the dogs trailing behind.

FRANK (V.O.)
Dear Dad. I'm retired now, living a quiet life in a small village in Europe. I hope you are doing well, and you're not mad at me for running away.

INT. - LAVALIER HOME. - NIGHT
The family is eating dinner together, and Frank looks surprised as Monique brings a birthday cake out from the kitchen. As everyone starts to sing....

FRANK (V.O.)
Yesterday was my 19th birthday, and when I blew out the candles, I wished that we could all be together, the three of us living in our old house in New Rochelle.

Frank blows out the candles, and everyone cheers. Monique walks over and turns on some music as Patrice opens another beer.

MONIQUE
Patrice, dance with me.

Monique and Patrice start to dance.

FRANK
Patrice, were you there when my father danced with my mother?

Patrice turns to Frank, a bit drunk.

PATRICE
Oh, yes. I saw the fireworks. I was only 12, but I knew what was going on.

FRANK
How did he do it?

PATRICE
Do what?

FRANK
With all those soldiers there, how did he do it? How did he convince her to marry him?

PATRICE
Convince? She didn't even speak English.

MONIQUE
Patrice. Please.

PATRICEs
What's the big secret? She didn't marry him because of the dancing.

Monique starts talking to Patrice in French.

PATRICE
He wants to know. He wants to know about his mother! His family!
(*back to Frank*)
She married him because of the baby. Is that so terrible?

Frank stares at Patrice, tries to understand what he's saying.

PATRICE
She was 16. They sat Paula down and said she had to marry your
father, told her she had no choice but to go home with him.

FRANK
And the baby?

MONIQUE
Patrice....enough!

PATRICE
The baby died a few days after it was born. I think it was a boy.
See, it's no big deal.

Patrice stands alone in the middle of the room.

PATRICE
Now who wants to dance?

EXT. - WAREHOUSE. - MONTRICHARD. - MORNING
The sun is coming up as Frank and Patrice walk up to the front of a
LARGE WAREHOUSE that sits near the center of town.

PATRICE
I hope you are good with your hands.

FRANK
I thought you made wine with your feet.

PATRICE
Wine? We don't make wine here.

FRANK
I thought wine was the family business.

PATRICE
No. There's no money in wine. The money is in the paper.

INT. - LAVALIER WAREHOUSE. - DAY
CLOSE ON: A PROFESSIONAL PRINTING PRESS, 90 FEET LONG,
10 FEET WIDE.

The giant machine fills the warehouse. TEN MEN work in the massive
press room, the deafening THUMP of the machine shaking the walls as
it struggles to spit out 10 COLOR PAGES a minute. WE SEE samples
of their work lining the walls — FRENCH NEWSPAPERS, COLOR
POSTERS, ADVERTISEMENTS.

CLOSE ON: FRANK staring up at the giant PRINTING PRESS, his
body limp, his face cold.

FRANK
This is the family business?

PATRICE
Printers. All of us. What do you
think? Terrible noise, right?

CLOSE ON: FRANK lost in his own
world, his mind racing as he stares at
every part of the machine — his eyes
cold with excitement and dread.

FRANK
Patrice...

Modesty is not one of my virtues.
At the time, virtue was not one of my
virtues.
—Frank W. Abagnale, from his book

PATRICE
It's hard to breathe. It's like a tomb — they can't have windows. Too much light will change the color...

Frank starts to back up toward the door, clearly about to get sick.

PATRICE
It's okay, I understand. This room is hell — you never get used to it.

INT. - LAVALIER HOUSE. - MONTRICHARD. - NIGHT
Frank reaches into the back of the closet and pulls out his PILOT'S UNI-FORM. As he slips on the jacket, Oliver walks in and turns on the light.

OLIVER
Frank... I'm scared.

FRANK
It's okay. You just had a bad dream. Go back to sleep.

Frank walks over to the bed with Oliver, tucks him in. He reaches into his bag, pulls out a small PAN AM MODEL AIRPLANE, and sets it on Oliver's nightstand.

INT. - LAVALIER HOME. - NIGHT
Frank is holding his suitcase as he makes his way through the dark house. Before he gets to the door, the sound of Monique's voice stops him.

MONIQUE
You are going home?

Monique is standing in the kitchen. Frank turns to her, slowly shakes his head "no."

MONIQUE
Then where are you going?

Frank slowly reaches up, puts his PILOT'S CAP on.

FRANK
I don't know.

INT. - PRINTING ROOM. - NIGHT
The PRINTING PRESS is thumping and grinding, the lights low, the press room empty except for Frank, who stands at one end of the machine, his shirt off, working like a man obsessed as he operates the massive press by himself — HUNDREDS OF PERFECT BLUE AND WHITE PAN AM CHECKS SLIDING OFF THE PAPER ROLLS AND DROPPING INTO THE TRAP.

EXT. - MONTRICHARD. - MORNING
Frank is walking through town in his Pilot's uniform, heading for the train station. Some kids are playing soccer, and the ball rolls toward Frank. He steps around it as he makes his way to the train station.

Frank Abagnale was a lonely and sometimes confused kid who was just looking for some kind of acceptance and entrance into the world. I think that is really quite poignant and universal. We can all remember being 17, 18, or 19 years old and thinking, how come I'm sitting here alone? Why aren't I part of something greater than my own creation?

—Tom Hanks

INT. - FBI OFFICE. - WASHINGTON
Carl Hanratty is sitting in his office trying to use a new electric pencil sharpener, which he has just taken out of the box. No matter what he does, the pencil remains dull. As Carl inspects the sharpener, Fox and Amdursky rush in holding an envelope, big smiles on their faces.

AMDURSKY
Carl... we got one.

Carl stands, the blood rushing back to his face.

HANRATTY
Where?

INT. - FBI OFFICES. - WASHINGTON, D.C. - DAY

Carl, Amdursky, and Fox are facing Assistant Director Marsh, a stack
of PAN AM checks on the desk in front of him.

HANRATTY
Singapore. Australia. South America. Egypt.

ASSISTANT DIRECTOR MARSH
Why wasn't I called?

HANRATTY
Nobody was called, Sir. The banks didn't know what was
happening until last week.

ASSISTANT DIRECTOR MARSH
That's impossible.

HANRATTY
They didn't call because he's not counterfeiting. It's something else.

ASSISTANT DIRECTOR MARSH
What's he doing?

HANRATTY
He's making real checks, Sir. These are so perfect, Pan Am couldn't
tell the difference.

Carl struggles to unfold a map across Marsh's desk.

HANRATTY
The last check was cashed in Madrid a week ago. My guess, he's
still there. We have to go now, Sir, today.

ASSISTANT DIRECTOR MARSH
Go where? Spain? You want to go to Spain?

HANRATTY
Eventually he'll have to go back to the spot where he printed those checks. I think that's why he's moving back through Europe. Look at the map — he's making a circle. He's running out of checks.

Marsh looks at the map one more time.

HANRATTY
I know it's a long shot, but if we could track him from Madrid...

Marsh slowly stands and grabs his coat.

HANRATTY
Sir, we can still catch him.

ASSISTANT DIRECTOR MARSH
I'm sorry, Carl. If you couldn't catch him here, you're not gonna catch him there.

INT. - CARL HANRATTY'S OFFICE. - DAY
A MAP OF EUROPE lies across the desk as Carl sits in his office staring down at a stack of Frank's PAN AM checks. He runs his hands across one of the checks, then grabs a photograph that shows one of Frank's FINGERPRINTS from the check.

He holds the fingerprint in his hand, staring down at it as if he were staring at Frank's.

INT. - PENNER AND SONS PRINTERS. - NEW YORK CITY. - DAY
Carl Hanratty is being led through the large, cluttered offices that house PENNER AND SONS PRINTERS. He passes walls of PRINTING SUPPLIES, SAMPLE CHECKS, COMPANY LOGOS, and a small, old-fashioned press.

TWO OLD MEN are sitting at a small wooden table staring up at Carl. They are ABE AND IRA PENNER, 70s — both in short sleeves, the two brothers smoking cigars as they use a backlight to examine the checks that Carl has presented to them.

ABE
It's a perfect one-sixteenth all the way around. Color separation is flawless — there's no bleeding.

IRA
Nobody does this kind of work in the States. Nobody but us.

HANRATTY
Where was it printed?

The TWO MEN look up at Carl.

ABE
It was printed on a monster — a Heidelberg — maybe an Istra — a dinosaur, four color. You can smell the weight — two tons without the ink.

HANRATTY
Where do they print like this?

IRA
Germany. Great Britain.

ABE
France.

EXT. - PENNER AND SONS PRINTERS. - ALLEY. - DAY
Hanratty walks outside with Fox and Amdursky.

HANRATTY
France? France. Frank's Mother said the name of a village in France where they didn't have Sara Lee. The village where she met Frank's father.

136

AMDURSKY
I don't remem...

HANRATTY
It started with an "M." "Mount" something. Mr. Fox —

Fox takes out a SMALL BLACK NOTEBOOK, starts flipping through the pages.

FOX
Question. "You met your husband during the war?"

HANRATTY
Tell me!

FOX
Answer. "Yes, I lived in a very small village in France. The kind of place where they've never heard of Sara Lee."

HANRATTY
Tell me you wrote down the name, Mr. Fox.

FOX
Mount Richard.

INT. - BAR. - DAY
CLOSE ON: A HAND HOLDING A DIME — DROPPING IT INTO THE JUKEBOX. WE HEAR DEAN MARTIN singing EVERYBODY LOVES SOMEBODY. Frank Abagnale Sr., dressed in his postman's uniform, dances himself back to the bar, sits at a stool under the TV and watches the news. The music is drowning out the NEWSCASTER.

HANRATTY
Looks like they caught him...

Frank Sr. turns around, sees Carl Hanratty standing behind him. Carl motions to the TV.

HANRATTY
The Boston Strangler. He tried to escape.

Carl takes a seat next to Frank Sr., who finishes his drink and starts to get up. He is clearly drunk.

FRANK SR.
I have to finish my route. The mail must go through.

HANRATTY
They fired you two months ago for pushing your supervisor.

FRANK SR.
He lied. It was just an argument — I never pushed anyone. They're gonna bring me back for the holidays.

HANRATTY
What was the argument about?

FRANK SR.
He doesn't believe we should be at war. So I told him to have some respect, that I was a Medal of Honor winner...

When people hear my story, they inevitably think it's fascinating and glamorous. In truth, it was a very, very lonely life. I was just a teenager. I missed my dad. I missed my mom. I never got to go to a prom or even a high school football game. I never had a relationship with anyone my own age. Everyone I knew was much older than me. I couldn't really have any friends because no one really knew me. In essence, I was deceiving everyone I met and that made it impossible to get really close to anyone.

My kids have grown up asking their mother why dad wakes up in the middle of the night and goes down to the TV room, but he doesn't watch television, he sits there all night.

There are things I can't forget, things I am not meant to forget. I think a lot about my father. He was a very, very loving man. What I remember most often about growing up is that every night my dad came into our bedrooms, all four of us kids, to kiss us goodnight. He was 6'3" and he would drop down on a knee, give me a kiss on the cheek, pull the cover up, and whisper in my ear, "I love you, I love you very much." That was the last thing we heard every night.

My father died while I was in prison, so I never got to see him again. I never got to tell him how much I loved him, how much I missed him.

I've lived my life and played the cards I was dealt, but it wasn't as glamorous as it may look in the movie.

I would never want to live that life again.

—Frank W. Abagnale, on the movie

HANRATTY
Is that the truth, Frank? Are you a Medal of Honor winner?

Frank stares at Carl, hesitates for a long BEAT. And then the truth hits him hard, as if he almost doesn't believe it himself.

FRANK SR.
Yes. I saved the the lives of four men in this little village. I gave the medal to my wife.

HANRATTY
What was the name of the village?

FRANK SR.
Maybe you should ask her.

HANRATTY
She won't speak to me. Her husband won't allow it.

FRANK SR.
I don't have to talk to you. I don't have to talk to anybody.

Carl reaches into his pocket and pulls out a $50 BILL. He places it on the bar in front of Frank Sr.

HANRATTY
What was the name of the village?

Frank Sr. stares down at the money, holds it tight in his hands.

HANRATTY
Come on, Frank, you can do this.

FRANK SR.
I'm his father.

HANRATTY
You think you can protect him?

FRANK SR.
You probably got a space on your wall all picked out, gonna have him stuffed and mounted. No, not my Frank, he's not going on any wall.

Hanratty takes out another 50, hands it to Frank Sr.

HANRATTY
Will you be there when he gets caught, Frank? Will you be there when he turns the wrong corner, walks into the wrong bank?

Frank Sr. stares down at the money.

HANRATTY
Look where you are. Look around. You can't save anyone from here.

Hanratty turns to leave, and Frank calls after him.

FRANK SR.
I was a hero. I gave her the medal instead of a ring.

This stops Hanratty.

FRANK SR.
She was this blonde angel — 200 soldiers were crammed into this tiny social hall to watch her dance. I turned to my buddies, and I told them all — I would not leave France without her.

HANRATTY
What was the name of the village?

Frank Sr. TEARS THE $50 BILL IN HALF, drops them on the floor and turns back to the bar.

FRANK SR.
Looks like I owe the government another hundred.

Hanratty waits for a BEAT, then turns and walks along the endless bar as he makes his way toward Fox and Amdursky, who are waiting at the door. Carl glances back at Frank Sr., who has taken his seat at the opposite end of the bar.

> **HANRATTY**
> Call the United States Army. Find out if Frank William Abagnale was really a Medal of Honor winner. Find out if he really saved the lives of four men.

> **FOX**
> And if he did?

> **HANRATTY**
> Tell me where it happened.

EXT. - MONTRICHARD. - CHRISTMAS EVE. - NIGHT
Church bells are ringing and the entire village is decorated with strings of Christmas lights. It's Christmas Eve, and everyone is moving toward Church — candles in hand for midnight mass.

INT. - LAVALIER PRINTING. - MONTRICHARD. - NIGHT
The massive ISTRA PRINTER is thumping in the windowless chamber — smoke rising from the gears as the two ton monster pushes itself — the paper flying through its rollers as page after page of CHECKS spins off the line.

ON A CHAIR WE SEE Frank's white shirt, black coat, and black pilot's hat — along with a large suitcase and two empty glass bottles of pop. A radio is on, Christmas music turned up high, unable to compete with the machine.

Frank is standing on a chair pouring water on the gears, his shirt off, his body moving along the side of the monster.

But then all of it stops — the gears lock, the rollers frozen and filled with paper.

The thumping machine quickly turns silent, stands motionless like a dead dragon. A STACK OF CHECKS fall from the trap — start to float down over the room — the paper falling like snow as Frank hops down from the machine.

As he starts to pick up the checks, he sees Carl Hanratty standing by the front of the press. He has hit the emergency shut-off switch, and is holding his own coat over his arms and hands. The room is hot, and Carl is sweating through his shirt, his body stiff as he stares at Frank.

> **HANRATTY**
> Frank...get yourself dressed. You're under arrest.

Frank slowly walks toward Carl.

> **FRANK**
> Hey, Carl. I'm starving. You want to get something to eat?

> **HANRATTY**
> Frank, right now there's two dozen French police officers outside that door. They wanted to bring you in without my help, without the help of an American, but I told them I wouldn't take them to you unless I could put the cuffs on.

Carl takes his hands out from under his jacket and tosses Frank a pair of handcuffs.

> **HANRATTY**
> Put those on. We have two minutes.

Frank looks at the handcuffs, then at Carl. He walks over to the chair, quickly puts on his shirt.

> **FRANK**
> Do you have a gun?

> **HANRATTY**
> No.

> **FRANK**
> And you say there's two dozen French police officers out there right now? On Christmas Eve?

Frank puts on his pilot's jacket and hat.

> **HANRATTY**
> Yes.

> **FRANK**
> There's no windows here. You mind if I take a peek out the door?

Frank moves toward the door.

> **HANRATTY**
> Frank, don't. I told them I'd walk out first and signal.

Frank stops at the door, looks back at Carl.

> **HANRATTY**
> Just put the cuffs on.

> **FRANK**
> I can't do that, Carl. Because I think you're lying. I don't think there's anybody out there.

> **HANRATTY**
> Frank, we don't have time.

> **FRANK**
> That's good — keep it up. Tell me what you want me to see.

> **HANRATTY**
> I wouldn't lie to you.

RIGHT: The real Frank Abagnale (center) appears in a cameo as a French police-man who arrests Leonardo DiCaprio's character in the film's final moments.

FRANK
You're wearing a wedding ring. You lied about that.

HANRATTY
You asked me if I had a family. I did. I don't anymore.

A PHONE RINGS, and Carl walks over and picks it up. He nervously talks into the receiver.

HANRATTY (INTO PHONE)
Yes. There's no problem. We're coming out now.

Carl hangs up the phone, and Frank can't help but smile.

FRANK
That was good. That was very good. Did you pay the hotel desk clerk a few dollars to make that call?

HANRATTY
That was Captain Luc. He says I have one minute to bring you out.

Frank puts a stack of checks in his suitcase and moves toward the door.

FRANK
You almost got me, Carl. Merry Christmas.

Frank is at the door when Carl rushes toward him.

HANRATTY
You have to trust me, Frank. These people have been embarrassed, they're angry. You rob their banks, you steal their money, you live in their country. I told you this would happen, that there was only one way for it to end, so don't make a mistake.

FRANK
Keep pushing, Carl. Keep pushing the lie until it's true.

HANRATTY
They will kill you. If you walk out that door, they will kill you.

FRANK
Is that the truth?

HANRATTY
Yes.

FRANK
Do you have any kids?

Carl hesitates before he answers.

HANRATTY
I have a four-year-old daughter.

FRANK
Do you swear on your daughter?

Carl slowly nods his head. Frank stares at him, then back to the handcuffs. He is trying to find the bluff in Carl's eyes, the one hint that will let him walk out the door. But there's nothing. He takes the handcuffs off the table, and he leans back against the wall — his body almost going limp.

FRANK
You can't do it, can you?

HANRATTY
Do what?

Frank walks back to the table, takes the handcuffs and cuffs his hands in front of him. Carl takes a deep breath, slowly moves toward the door.

FRANK
Carl, how mad are they?

EXT. - LAVALIER PRINT SHOP. - NIGHT
Carl walks out first, waving his arms in the air as Frank walks out behind him. The two men take a few steps, and then stand frozen at the door, staring out at the village in front of them. A thin smile comes over Frank's face as he STARES OUT AT THE EMPTY STREETS — THE ENTIRE VILLAGE DESERTED.

FRANK
Carl, that was really good.

After a long BEAT WE HEAR the cocking of weapons — and then WE SEE IT — THE ROOFTOPS ARE FILLED WITH FRENCH POLICE OFFICERS — ALL OF THEM HOLDING GUNS AND RIFLES, THE ENTIRE PRINT SHOP BUILDING SURROUNDED.

HANRATTY
It's okay! I got him!

THE COPS START SCREAMING IN FRENCH AS SQUAD CARS CONVERGE ON THE SCENE, POLICE OFFICERS GRABBING FRANK AND THROWING HIM INTO THE BACK OF A CAR — HANRATTY GETTING PUSHED ASIDE.

HANRATTY
What are you doing? Let me in the car! I'm going with him! I'm supposed to go with him!

THE SQUAD CAR SPEEDS OFF — LEAVING CARL STRANDED IN THE MIDDLE OF THE ROAD — THE CAR SHOOTING THROUGH TOWN AND JOINING A CONVOY OF OTHER POLICE CARS.

SIRENS WAIL AS THE ENTIRE VILLAGE STARTS TO COME OUT OF CHURCH TO SEE THE COMMOTION, THE PEOPLE MOVING PAST CARL HANRATTY AS IF HE WEREN'T EVEN THERE.

EXT. - PERPIGNAN PRISON. - DAY
SUPER: FRANCE, DECEMBER 25, 1969

Carl Hanratty has a look of sheer determination on his face as he walks out of the prison with Frank, who is handcuffed and shackled.

Amdursky and Fox meet them at the gate.

INT. - TWA AIRPLANE. - DAY
Frank and Carl Hanratty are sitting next to each other in the back of the plane. Through the window Frank can see the skyline of Manhattan. Amdursky and Fox are smoking in the aisle.

> **FRANK**
> Carl, you have to let me call my father when we land. I want to talk to him before he sees me on television.

> **HANRATTY**
> Your father is dead, Frank. I'm sorry. I didn't want to say anything until we were closer to home.

Frank turns to Carl.

> **HANRATTY**
> He was in Grand Central Station, trying to catch a train, and he fell down some steps. I didn't want to be the one to tell you.

> **FRANK**
> You're lying. You said I could call him.

> **HANRATTY**
> He broke his neck. I'm sorry.

> **FRANK**
> Who are you to say that? Who are you to say something like that!? You told me I could call him!

> **HANRATTY**
> The police report said he had been drinking.

> **FRANK**
> Carl, I'm gonna be sick. I have to use the bathroom.

Carl quickly takes off Frank's handcuffs, and he jumps from his seat and runs into the bathroom. Carl stands in the aisle with Amdursky and Fox.

INT. - AIRPLANE BATHROOM. - MOMENTS LATER
Frank is standing in the tiny bathroom, tears running down his face as he stares at himself in the mirror.

FLASHBACK INT. - FRANK'S HOUSE. - NEW ROCHELLE. - DAY
Frank Sr. is standing behind his son, SHOWING HIM HOW TO TIE HIS TIE. Paula is standing in front of Frank, smiling as she watches her two men.

> **FRANK SR.**
> And then you go around, and under. It's almost like the long end is chasing the short end.

INT. - AIRPLANE BATHROOM -
Frank slowly reaches up, pulls the tie from around his neck. He reaches into his pocket, pulls out a DIME.

INT. - AIRPLANE. - MINUTES LATER
Carl Hanratty checks his watch as a FLIGHT ATTENDANT walks past him and smiles.

> **FLIGHT ATTENDANT**
> You'll have to take your seat, Sir. I've told you twice, we're landing.

Carl knocks on the bathroom door. Then he tries to open it.

> **HANRATTY**
> Frank? Come on, Frank, open the door! Damn it...Frank!

> **AMDURSKY**
> What do we do?

> **HANRATTY**
> Break it down.

Amdursky starts kicking at the bathroom door, slamming his heel against the metal release. The door breaks free, and the three men stares in disbelief at the EMPTY BATHROOM.

Carl looks down, sees the DIME sitting by the base of the toilet. As he reaches down, he sees that all of the TOILET SCREWS have been loosened.

Carl grabs the toilet, and quickly lifts the entire TOILET UNIT off the floor. He looks straight down into the thin white crawlspace that leads straight down — THE HATCH HELD OPEN BY A THIN BLACK TIE.

EXT. - PLANE. - MOMENTS LATER
The plane has landed and stopped short on the runway. WE SEE Frank crawling through a HATCH near the landing gear. He drops 15 feet to the ground below, starts running across the runway.

INT. - PLANE. - MOMENTS LATER
All of the passengers remain seated as Carl, Amdursky, and Fox come running from the bathroom.

> **HANRATTY**
> Everyone stay seated. We're FBI — someone get the door open!

As Carl starts moving through the plane toward the door, something outside the window catches his eye. He sees Frank sprinting across the tarmac, making his way toward the terminal.

> **HANRATTY**
> God in heaven...

EXT. - PAULA'S HOUSE. - LONG ISLAND. - NIGHT.
Frank looks exhausted as he gets out of a CAB and runs up the drive- way of a large, one story house, BANGING ON THE FRONT DOOR and then moving toward the side windows. A Cadillac sits in the drive- way covered in ice.

The windows are fogged from the snow, and Frank can only make out shapes and colors — a fireplace — a red chair — a Christmas tree. He stares through the glass for a BEAT — and is STARTLED BY A FACE that suddenly appears in the window. The face is a LITTLE GIRL — not even four years old — smiling as she blows into a harmonica — her eyes never looking down at him.

> **FRANK**
> What's your name? What's your name?

And then she suddenly stops — as if she were called away. WE HEAR SIRENS WAILING IN THE DISTANCE as Frank rushes back to the front door — sees Jack Barnes standing by the open door.

> **FRANK**
> I need to see my Mother.

Jack stares at him for a BEAT, then moves aside as Frank rushes into the house.

INT. PAULA'S HOUSE. - LONG ISLAND. - NIGHT.
Frank rushes through the house, finds his mother sitting in the living room staring into the fireplace. Lights from the Christmas tree fill the room with a warm glow, and there are holiday cookies sitting on a sil- ver platter. The sirens are getting closer now as Frank rushes toward his mother, who is crying.

> **FRANK**
> They lied to me about Dad. They lied about everything.

> **PAULA**
> Jack...please take her upstairs.

Jack picks up his daughter, carries her upstairs as the little girl continues to play the harmonica.

FRANK
Tell me what happened to him.

PAULA
I really don't know.

FRANK
What happened, Mom? Tell me what happened? Why did you divorce him? Why did you do that to him!

PAULA
There are things you wouldn't understand.

FRANK
Just tell me the truth. He saw you dance, right!?

PAULA
I was a kid when I met your father.

FRANK
He saw you on stage — he was the one!

PAULA
I didn't even speak English —

In a way I related to the chutzpah of what Abagnale did because it reminded me of when I pretended to be an executive as a teenager, wearing a suit and walking past the guard at Universal Studios. In a way, I lived a double life, hanging around that summer to see how movies and TV shows got made.

—Steven Spielberg

FRANK
Two hundred men in that social hall —

PAULA
He got me pregnant.

Paula turns away from her son and lights a cigarette.

PAULA
I was 18, and my parents said I had to marry him.

FRANK
No, you're wrong...

PAULA
The baby was born too soon. The nurses knew he was going to die, so they kept telling me to hold him.

FRANK
You're telling it all wrong!

PAULA
I was scared the baby would die in my arms, so I said no. Can you imagine that, Frank? I didn't want to hold my own son.

THE SIRENS ARE DEAFENING NOW — THE LIGHTS AND SOUNDS FROM THE POLICE CARS FILLING THE HOUSE — THE DRIVEWAY AND FRONT LAWN FLOODED WITH POLICE AND FBI CARS —

Paula slowly stands, leads Frank over to the couch and sits him down. She covers him with a blanket — then kisses him on the head —

PAULA
You go to sleep now, Frank. Please just try and close your eyes and go to sleep.

He slowly reaches out, is about to take the cigarette from her mouth. His hand moves past the cigarette and touches her face.

Paula turns and walks away, slowly moving up the stairs as Frank sits back on the couch, alone in the massive living room, the lights and

shadows criss-crossing across his face as he lies back and closes his eyes.

WE PAN across the Christmas tree and fireplace and through the front window — where Carl Hanratty is leading 20 armed men up the long drive.

INT. - MAXIMUM SECURITY PRISON. - ATLANTA

Frank stands in front of his cell in the isolation wing of the prison.

> **JUDGE (V.O.)**
> Taking into account the gravity of these crimes, your history of bold and elusive behavior and your complete lack of respect for the laws of the United States, I have no choice but to ignore your request to be treated as a minor — and sentence you to twelve years in Atlanta's maximum security prison, and recommend strongly that you be kept in isolation for the entirety of that sentence.

There are no bars, no windows, just square, individual cell boxes. Frank walks into his cell, the door closing behind him.

INT. - PRISON VISITING ROOM. - DAY

Frank is wearing his prison jumpsuit as he's led into the visitor's room and placed in a chair that faces bulletproof glass. Carl Hanratty is sitting across from him. They both pick up their phones.

> **HANRATTY**
> Merry Christmas, Frank.

Frank doesn't answer him.

> **HANRATTY**
> I got some comic books here.

An awkward moment as Carl puts the comics on the floor.

> **HANRATTY**
> They say the first year inside is the hardest.

> **FRANK**
> You caught me. What do you want?

> **HANRATTY**
> I don't know. Maybe this was a bad idea. I'll go.

As Carl starts to put the phone down.

> **FRANK**
> What's your daughter's name?

> **HANRATTY**
> Grace. She lives in Chicago with her mother. I don't get to see her much.

Frank stares at Carl for a BEAT.

> **FRANK**
> What's in the briefcase?

A Federal judge sentenced me to twelve years in Federal prison. I served about four years in a prison outside of Washington, D.C. When I was 26, the government decided to parole me on two conditions.

One was that I go to Houston, Texas. Usually, you are paroled back to where you came from, but I had never been to Texas.

Two was that I go to work helping the government deal with these crimes of forgery and counterfeiting. I wouldn't be compensated, but that would be part of my parole. So, in Houston, I worked lots of menial odd jobs to support myself while I taught law enforcement officers.

Being the opportunist I always was, I started to realize that if these law enforcement people didn't know what I was teaching, then what did the banks know? What did companies know about fraud and counterfeiting? Why wasn't I out there telling banks and companies how to protect themselves and charging a fee for that information?

I negotiated a deal with the government where I'd continue working with the FBI if the government allowed me to also teach others.

I have done that for 25 years. I still work today with the FBI and still teach at the FBI Academy. The government still does not pay me or reimburse my travel expense, now, by my own choice. I travel on behalf of my government about fifty days a year. This is just my small way of paying back my debt.

Over the years, I have built my own consulting business. I have worked for 65 percent of the Fortune 500 countries in America. I've worked for all of the 50 largest banks in America. I've developed technology today that's found on just about every driver's license, car title, birth certificate, passport, and currency around the world.

—Frank W. Abagnale, on the film

HANRATTY
I'm on my way to the airport. I'm tracking a paperhanger who's working his way through Minnesota. This guy is driving me crazy.

FRANK
Do you have any of the checks?

Carl hesitates, then opens his briefcase and takes out a CHECK. He holds it against the glass.

HANRATTY
This is a counterfeit from Great Lakes Savings and Loan. You can see that he's using a...

FRANK
It's a teller at the bank.

HANRATTY
What?

FRANK
It's a teller. Every bank uses hand stamps for the dates. They get used over and over, so they're always worn down, and the numbers are always cracking — the sixes and nines go first. Look at the numbers in the corner — the ink is worn flat, the nines and sixes are cracking — that's the stamp of a teller, Carl. Looks like you got yourself an inside job.

INT. - PRISON. - NIGHT
Frank is lying in his cell, staring into the darkness.

FRANK
Ladies and gentleman, we are leveled off at 35,000 feet. The smoking signs have been turned off for those of you in the designated

smoking section. Our flight time will be five hours and thirty-seven minutes. The weather on arrival is good with clear skies and balmy temperatures. My name is Captain Frank Taylor — so just sit back, relax, and enjoy our flight to Honolulu.

INT. - JAIL CELL. - ATLANTA PRISON. - DAY

The prison is locked down.

Carl Hanratty and Assistant Director Marsh are passing rows of cells as they make their way through the prison.

INT. - INTERROGATION ROOM. - DAY

Frank is sitting across from Carl and Assistant Director Marsh, a glass of milk in front of him. TWO GUARDS stand behind him with rifles. Frank is 26 years old, but still has the boyish face of a teenager.

> **FRANK**
> Carl, one of these days you should get yourself a new jacket. What is that material?

Frank touches Carl's jacket.

> **HANRATTY**
> Cashmere.

> **FRANK**
> That isn't cashmere — look at the lining. It's some kind of polyester. You should see my tailor in New York.

> **ASSISTANT DIRECTOR MARSH**
> Mr. Abagnale, you've served four years of an 18-year sentence.

> **FRANK**
> That's right. Four years, two months.

> **ASSISTANT DIRECTOR MARSH**
> I'd like you to look at something for me, tell me what you think.

Director Marsh takes an envelope out of a briefcase, slides it over to Frank. Frank opens the envelope and pulls out a PAYROLL CHECK. He holds the check in his hand, never looks at it.

> **FRANK**
> It's a fake.

> **ASSISTANT DIRECTOR MARSH**
> How do you know? You haven't looked at it.

> **FRANK**
> There's no perforated edge, which means this check was hand cut, not fed. The paper is double bonded, much too heavy for a bank check. The magnetic ink is raised against my fingers instead of flat.

Frank brings the check to his nose, sniffs it.

> **FRANK**
> This doesn't smell like MICR. It's probably drafting ink, the kind you buy at a stationery store.

Carl and Director Marsh exchange a look.

> **ASSISTANT DIRECTOR MARSH**
> Frank, would you be interested in working with the FBI's Financial Crimes Unit?

> **FRANK**
> I already have a job here. I deliver the mail.

> **HANRATTY**
> No, Frank. We'd get you out.

> **FRANK**
> Why are you saying this? You caught me, isn't that enough? Why can't you leave me alone?

There is a redemptive feeling to the end of this movie. In my opinion this story is an excellent example of someone who has served his time but has something to offer in terms of assisting law enforcement. There is a saving grace to the fact that the FBI in this instance reached out to Frank and co-opted his abilities to assist in helping them combat future check fraud and check counterfeiting.

In fact, the real Frank Abagnale has turned his life completely around. He has formed an association with other agents, particular those at the FBI Academy where Frank volunteers his time to give seminars to new agents and train agents in the financial crimes area. So he is assisting in the war against the type of violation that he himself committed. This proves that there is redemption after all.

—William J. Rehder,
FBI Technical Advisor

ASSISTANT DIRECTOR MARSH
Frank, we have the power to take you out of prison. You'd be placed in the custody of the FBI, where you'd serve the remainder of your sentence as an employee of the federal government.

FRANK
Whose custody?

HANRATTY
Mine.

INT. - FBI FIELD OFFICE. - WASHINGTON, D.C. - DAY
SUPER: MARCH, 1975

Frank wears a brand new black suit as he walks into the massive FBI BUILDING. He approaches a SECURITY GUARD.

FRANK
I'm Frank Abagnale. I'm supposed to start work here today.

INT. - FBI BUILDING. - THIRD FLOOR. - DAY
Frank makes his way down a long hallway, passing other young men in

dark suits who have come out of their offices to see him pass. Frank sees Carl Hanratty standing at the end of the hall.

> **FRANK**
> Morning, Carl.

Frank turns and stares at a door marked FRAUD. He casually walks inside. Hanratty walks to the door, stares in at Frank, who looks uncomfortable as he stands behind an empty desk.

> **FRANK**
> How long do I have to stay here?

> **HANRATTY**
> Well, it's nine-to-five.

> **FRANK**
> No. I mean how long?

> **HANRATTY**
> Every day, Frank. Every day until we let you go.

INT. - FRANK'S FBI OFFICE. - DAY

A stack of files sit on Frank's desk. There are hundreds of MUG SHOTS, PILES OF COUNTERFEIT CHECKS. Frank looks out the window of his office, stares out at the WASHINGTON SKYLINE.

INT. - HANRATTY'S OFFICE. - FBI. - DAY

Carl is working at his desk. Frank walks in and closes the door behind him.

> **HANRATTY**
> This is a bad time, Frank. I'm clearing my desk for the weekend.

> **FRANK**
> Would it be okay if I went to work with you tomorrow?

Carl stops for a BEAT, looks up at Frank.

> **HANRATTY**
> Tomorrow is Saturday. I'm flying to Chicago to see my daughter. But I'll be back at work on Monday.

> **FRANK**
> Carl...what do I do until Monday?

> **HANRATTY**
> I can't help you there, kid.

INT. - FBI OFFICES. - DAY

Frank sits alone eating a sandwich, looking through a BOOK OF MUG SHOTS. He stops when he sees his own MUG SHOT, the black and white picture staring up at him.

Frank carefully rips the mug shot out of the book and puts it in his pocket.

EXT. - WASHINGTON D.C. - DAY

Frank is walking the streets, carrying a small bag of groceries as he makes his way home. Something in a STORE WINDOW catches his eye, and Frank stands frozen on the corner, looking across at a WINDOW DISPLAY.

CLOSE ON: THE WINDOW OF A COSTUME SHOP.

There are several MANNEQUINS dressed in different costumes. Frank slowly approaches the window, stares at a mannequin wearing an AIRLINE PILOT'S UNIFORM.

INT. - WASHINGTON AIRPORT DEPARTURE TUNNEL. - NIGHT

Frank is wearing the PILOT'S UNIFORM as he walks through the endless tunnel that leads to the departure gates. A VOICE from behind stops him.

HANRATTY
How did you do it, Frank? How did you pass the bar exam in Louisiana?

Frank never turns around. He continues to make his way toward the gate.

HANRATTY
Did you know I was recruited by the FBI while I was still in law school? The government said I was the best the country had to offer, top of my class — and they chased me until I said yes.

Frank finally stops, slowly turns to Carl.

FRANK
I'm sorry.

HANRATTY
I spent four years arranging your release. I convinced the FBI, the Attorney General of the United States that you wouldn't run.

Frank starts to walk again, and Carl stays with him.

HANRATTY
You go back to Europe, and you'll die in Perpignan. You try and run here in the States, and we'll send you back to Atlanta for 50 years.

FRANK
I never asked for your help.

HANRATTY
Please, Frank, you leave and I'm finished. I got you out, I convinced them to let you out.

FRANK
Why did you do it?

HANRATTY
You're just a kid.

FRANK
I'm not your kid. What are you doing here? Why didn't you go to Chicago?

HANRATTY
My daughter can't see me this weekend. She's going skiing.

FRANK
You said she was four.

HANRATTY
She was four when I left. She's 15 now. My wife has been remarried for 11 years. I see Grace a couple times a year.

FRANK
I don't understand.

HANRATTY
Sure you do, Frank. Sometimes it's easier to live the lie.

Frank slowly turns and walks toward the EASTERN AIRLINES ticket counter.

HANRATTY
I'm gonna let you fly tonight. I won't even try and stop you because I know you'll be back on Monday.

FRANK
Why would I come back?

HANRATTY
Look around, Frank. Nobody is chasing you.

Frank stares at Carl for a long BEAT.

FRANK
Two mice fell in a bucket of cream. The
first mouse gave up and drowned, but
the second mouse struggled so hard he
churned that cream into butter — and he
crawled out. My father taught me that.

HANRATTY
Your father didn't get out. I hope you will.

Frank turns to the girl at the ticket counter.

FRANK
Hello, Amanda, is the jump-seat open on
the 10:30 to New York?

You want to see these people end
up happy. I think there's just no doubt
that, at the end of the day, Frank
Abagnale is a happy man. Certainly,
he's much happier now than he would
have been if he was still trying to steal
a couple of thousand dollars out of an
ATM machine. The movie accurately
reflects the happiness he found in life.
—Tom Hanks

Carl watches as Frank walks through a door
marked CREW ONLY, casually making his way toward the plane.

INT. WASHINGTON AIRPORT. - JETWAY/DOOR OF PLANE. - DAY
Frank is about to walk onto the plane. Just as he's about to cross
through the door, he stops himself — his eyes looking at the opening.
He's about to turn back when a STEWARDESS touches his arm.

STEWARDESS
Excuse me, Sir. Are you my deadhead?

INT. - CARL HANRATTY'S OFFICE. - DAY
Carl sits at his desk drinking coffee. He checks his watch, then calls out
to his SECRETARY.

HANRATTY
Is Abagnale in yet?

SECRETARY
No.

INT. - FBI OFFICE CONFERENCE ROOM. - DAY
Carl Hanratty is using the slide projector and standing in front of 10
AGENTS, including Special Agent Witkins.

HANRATTY
Good morning. I've called this briefing to discuss a check fraud and
counterfeiter who's been hitting banks all over Arizona.

A DOOR OPENS, and Carl looks to the back of the room, watches as
AGENT FOX walks in with a cup of coffee.

FOX
Sorry I'm late.

INT. - FBI OFFICE. - DAY
The office is packed with agents. Carl is working at the evidence desk,
sitting alone as he examines a stack of checks.

FRANK
You mind if I take a look?

Carl looks up, sees Frank standing over him. He motions to the chair
next to him, and Frank sits down as Carl slides over a check.

HANRATTY
Cashed in Houston a week ago. Cost the bank $16,000.

FRANK
It's a real check.

HANRATTY
It's been washed. The only thing that's been changed is the name of
the payee.

FRANK
It's perfect. This can't be bleach or hydrochloride.

HANRATTY
You're right. He found something new. Cutex nail polish remover — the acetone lifts the ink without a...

Carl stares at Frank, as serious as we've ever seen him.

HANRATTY
How did you do it, Frank? How did you cheat on the bar exam in Louisiana?

FRANK
I didn't cheat. I studied for two weeks, and I passed.

HANRATTY
Is that the truth, Frank? Is that the truth?

The two men look at each other for a long BEAT.

FRANK
I'll bet this guy is stealing the checks out of mailboxes — washing off the names and putting on his own — then if it were me, I'd call the bank and ask about the balance — make sure there's enough money to make it worth my while. This guy's pretty smart, Carl. I guess all we have to do is catch him...

AS FRANK AND CARL CONTINUE TO TALK, THE CAMERA STARTS TO RISE, STAYING ON THEM AS THEY SIT TOGETHER IN THE MIDDLE OF THE OFFICE — THE TWO MEN STARTING TO BLEND IN WITH THE OTHER AGENTS WHO ARE WORKING IN THE HUGE OFFICE — THE CAMERA SLOWLY LOSING THEM AS THEY DISAPPEAR INTO A SEA OF DARK SUITS.

INT. - GAME SHOW SET. - DAY
CLOSE ON: Frank Abagnale's face as we hear Joe Garagiola's voice.

JOE GARAGIOLA
Okay panel, you did a wonderful job. But now it's time to see who was telling the truth. So would the real Frank Abagnale Jr. please stand up?

TITLE CARD #1
Frank Abagnale Jr. has been married for 25 years. He has three sons and lives a quiet life in the Midwest.

Since his release from prison in 1974, Frank has helped the FBI capture some of the world's most elusive check forgers and counterfeiters, and is considered one of the world's foremost authorities on bank fraud and forgery.

Frank has also developed many of the secure checks that banks and Fortune 500 companies use every day. He holds several patents on these checks, and is paid a royalty every time one is printed.

These check royalties pay Frank Abagnale Jr. millions of dollars a year.

TITLE CARD #2
Special agent Carl Hanratty retired in 1986, having been awarded three distinguished service awards from the FBI. Frank Abagnale has four.

They remain close friends to this day.

THE END.

What I did 30 years ago is now

really 800 times easier to do because of the available technology. For example, when I had to forge a check, I literally had to create that check. I needed a four-color printing press that cost about a quarter of a million dollars. I had to learn how to do color separations, negatives, plates, typesetting, and much more. It took me months to create those documents.

Today, you can sit down at a computer at home and create the fanciest check in the world; print the fanciest stocks, bonds, and certificates with the technology available on a PC or a color copier or a scanner or digitizer.

—Frank W. Abagnale, on the movie

DREAMWORKS PICTURES PRESENTS

A KEMP COMPANY AND
SPLENDID PICTURES PRODUCTION

A PARKES/MacDONALD PRODUCTION

A STEVEN SPIELBERG FILM

LEONARDO DiCAPRIO

TOM HANKS

CATCH ME IF YOU CAN

CHRISTOPHER WALKEN
MARTIN SHEEN
NATHALIE BAYE
AMY ADAMS
JAMES BROLIN
BRIAN HOWE
FRANK JOHN HUGHES
STEVE EASTIN
CHRIS ELLIS
JOHN FINN

CASTING BY
DEBRA ZANE, CSA

CASTING ASSOCIATE **TERRI TAYLOR**

CO-PRODUCER
DEVORAH MOOS-HANKIN

BASED UPON THE BOOK BY
FRANK W. ABAGNALE
WITH STAN REDDING

TITLES BY
KUNTZEL + DEYGAS

MUSIC BY
JOHN WILLIAMS

COSTUME DESIGNER
MARY ZOPHRES

FILM EDITOR
MICHAEL KAHN, A.C.E.

PRODUCTION DESIGNER
JEANNINE OPPEWALL

DIRECTOR OF PHOTOGRAPHY
JANUSZ KAMINSKI, ASC

CO-EXECUTIVE PRODUCER
DANIEL LUPI

EXECUTIVE PRODUCERS
BARRY KEMP
LAURIE MacDONALD

EXECUTIVE PRODUCERS
MICHEL SHANE
TONY ROMANO

PRODUCED BY
STEVEN SPIELBERG
WALTER F. PARKES

SCREENPLAY BY
JEFF NATHANSON

DIRECTED BY
STEVEN SPIELBERG

156

Associate Producer
SERGIO MIMICA-GEZZAN

Unit Production Manager
CRISTEN CARR STRUBBE

First Assistant Director
SERGIO MIMICA-GEZZAN

Second Assistant Director
DAVID H. VENGHAUS, JR.

CAST

Frank Abagnale Jr. . . . **LEONARDO DiCAPRIO**
Carl Hanratty . . . . **TOM HANKS**
Frank Abagnale . . . . **CHRISTOPHER WALKEN**
Roger Strong . . . . **MARTIN SHEEN**
Paula Abagnale . . . . **NATHALIE BAYE**
Brenda Strong . . . . **AMY ADAMS**
Jack Barnes . . . . **JAMES BROLIN**
Tom Fox . . . . **BRIAN HOWE**
Earl Amdursky . . . **FRANK JOHN HUGHES**
Paul Morgan . . . . **STEVE EASTIN**
Special Agent Wilkes . . . . **CHRIS ELLIS**
Assistant Director Marsh . . . . **JOHN FINN**
Cheryl Ann . . . . **JENNIFER GARNER**
Carol Strong . . . . **NANCY LENEHAN**
Marci . . . . **ELLEN POMPEO**
Lucy . . . . **ELIZABETH BANKS**
Warden Garren . . . . **GUY THAUVETTE**
Darcy . . . . **CANDICE AZZARA**
Loan Officer . . . . **MATTHEW KIMBROUGH**
Football Player . . . . **JOSHUA BOYD**
Joanna . . . . **KAITLIN DOUBLEDAY**
Girl #1 . . . . **KELLY McNAIR**
Student #1 . . . . **JONATHAN DANKER**
Teacher . . . . **MAGGIE MELLIN**
Principal Evans . . . . **THOMAS KOPACHE**
Ms. Davenport . . . . **MARGARET TRAVOLTA**
Bartender . . . . **JIMMIE F. SKAGGS**
Men . . . . . **IAN BARFORD, RYAN CUTRONA**
Mr. Kesner . . . . **ALEX HYDE-WHITE**
Mrs. Lavalier . . . . **LILYAN CHAUVIN**
Ticket Clerk . . . . **EUGENE FLEMING**
Hotel Manager . . . . **ROBERT RUTH**
Ashley . . . . **JENNIFER MANLEY**
Pilot . . . . **JAMES MORRISON**
Bellman . . . . **ALEXANDER FOLK**
Mr. Rosen . . . . **ROBERT SYMONDS**
Female Bank Teller . . . . **JENNIFER KAN**
Front Desk Clerk . . **ROBERT CURTIS BROWN**
Young Female Teller . . . . **KELLY HUTCHINSON**
Manager . . . . **STEVE WITTING**
TWA Pilot . . . . **PHIL REEVES**
Receptionist . . . . . . **WENDY WORTHINGTON**
TWA Ticket Agent . . . . **JANE BODLE**
Auctioneer . . . . **J. PATRICK McCORMACK**
Motel Owner . . . . **BRIAN GOODMAN**
Salesman . . . . **RAY PROSCIA**
Riverbend Women . . . . . **SARAH LANCASTER**
JILL MATSON
Terry . . . . **MIKE BALDRIDGE**
Party Guy . . . . **JOEL EWING**
Young Doctor . . . . . . **RITCHIE MONTGOMERY**
Victor Griffith . . . . **JIM ANTONIO**
Party Girl . . . . **ANGELA SORENSEN**
Dr. Ashland . . . . **JONATHAN BRENT**
Emergency Nurse . . . . **BENITA KRISTA NALL**
Doctor Harris . . . . **SHANE EDELMAN**
Young Patient . . . . **ANDREW MEEKS**
FBI Agent . . . . **MORGAN RUSLER**
Bar Examiner . . . . . **JANE EDITH WILSON**
Judge . . . . **DAVE HAGER**
Kid . . . . **KYLE DAVIS**
Mr. Hendricks . . . . **PATRICK T. O'BRIEN**

Monica . . . . **JAIME RAY NEWMAN**
Heather . . . . **MERCEDES CORNETT**
Miggy . . . . **AMY ACKER**
FBI Agents . . . . **ROBERT PETERS**
JAMES DUMONT, THOMAS CRAWFORD
Secretary . . . . **SARAH RUSH**
Abe Penner . . . . **MALACHI THRONE**
Ira Penner . . . . **ALFRED DENNIS**
TWA Stewardess . . . . **DONNA KIMBALL**
Captain Oliver . . . . **JAN MUNROE**
Pilots **STEPHEN DUNHAM, BRANDON KEENER**
Little Girl . . . . . **JASMINE JESSICA ANTHONY**
NY Savings Bank Manager **ANTHONY POWERS**
Female Teller . . . . **LAUREN COHN**
Teen Waiter . . . . **JEREMY HOWARD**
Man #3 . . . . **JACK KNIGHT**
Ilene . . . . **JAMIE ANDERSON**
Candy . . . . **KAM HESKIN**
Daphne . . . . **NATALIE COMPAGNO**
Hotel Maid . . . . **ANA MARIA QUINTANA**
FBI Agent . . . . **GERALD MOLEN**
Little Girl on Street . . . . . . **CELINE DU TERTRE**
Blind Man . . . . **STAN BLY**
Young Man . . . . **JAMIE MOSS**
Peggy . . . . **JESSICA COLLINS**
Starr . . . . **AMY RYDELL**
French Policeman . . . . **FRANK W. ABAGNALE**
Prison Guard . . . . **ROGER LÈGER**
French Police
Captain . . . . . **JEAN-FRANÇOIS BLANCHARD**
French Police . . . . . . **MATHIEU GAUDREAULT**
GUY DANIEL TREMBLAY, ALEXANDRE
BISPING, PATRICE DUSSAULT
Maitre D' . . . . **PAUL TODD**
Kid . . . . **JAKE WAGNER**
Party Twins . **ASHLEY COHEN, KELLY COHEN**
Penner Brother #3 . . . . **MAX J. KERSTEIN**
Piano Player/Singer . . . . **ELLIS HALL**
Piano Player . . . . **STEVEN MEIZLER**
Co-Pilot . . . . **FRED DATIG**
Joe Garagiola . . . . **HIMSELF**
Airport Kid . . . . **RYAN KOTLER**
Choir . . . . **DOMINIC BOND, JEAN-FRANÇOIS**
BROUSSEAU, FRANCIS CAMPEAU,
RAPHAËL CARDIN, MARC-ANTOINE CÔTÉ,
ANTOINE DROLET-DUMOULIN, LÉON
DUSSAULT-GAGNÉ, SIMON HOULE-GAUTHIER,
VINCENT GÉNÉTREUX, SÉBASTIEN JEAN,
PASCAL LAROUCHE, WILLIAM LAUZON,
FLORENT LEGAULT, JASON McNALLY,
JULIEN NORMANDEAU, DAVID PARENT-
LALIBERTÉ, ALEXANDRE PEPIN,
NICOLAS RADESCHI, JONATHAN RENÉ,
SAMUEL ST-AMOUR
Stunt Coordinator . . . . . . **WEBSTER WHINERY**
Stunt Coordinator – Canada **MARC DÉSOURDY**
Stunts . . . . **MICHAEL ADAMS,**
DANNY AIELLO III, BILL ANAGNOS,
JOHN BAL, ALAIN BEDARD, JOE BOX,
PAUL BUCOSSI, PETER BUCOSSI,
EDWARD CONNA, JEANNINE EPPER,
ROY FARFEL, FRANK FERRARA,
BENÔIT GAUTHIER, ANDRÉ LAPERRIERE,
STÉPHANE LEFEBVRE, TOM MORGA,
MICK O'ROURKE, JANET PAPARAZZO,
DON PICARD, JODI PYNN, NORMAN ROY,
MIKE RUSSO, JIM VICKERS, BRIAN J. WILLIAMS

CREW

Art Director . . . . **SARAH KNOWLES**
Assistant Art Director . . . . **JOHN WARNKE**
Set Decorator . . . . **LESLIE A. POPE**
Camera Operator . . . . **MITCH DUBIN**

First Assistant Camera . . . . **STEVEN MEIZLER**
Second Assistant Camera . . . . . **TOM JORDAN**
Steadicam/B Camera
    Operator . . . . **DAVID EMMERICHS**
B First Assistant Camera . . . . . . **MARK SPATH**
Camera Loader . . . . **PAUL TOOMEY**
Camera Intern . . . . . . **SZYMON KACZMAREK**
Still Photographer **ANDREW COOPER, S.M.P.S.P.**
Script Supervisor . . . . **ANA MARIA QUINTANA**
Production Sound Mixer . . . **RONALD JUDKINS**
Boom Operator . . . . **ROBERT JACKSON**
Sound Technician . . . . **PEGGY NAMES**
Video Assist . . . . **DANIEL P. MOORE**
Supervising Sound
    Editors . . . .**CHARLES L. CAMPBELL**
                   JOHN A. LARSEN
Re-Recording Mixers . . . . **ANDY NELSON**
                   ANNA BEHLMER
First Assistant Editors . . . . . . **PATRICK CRANE**
                  RICHARD BYARD
Assistant Editor . . . . **MICHAEL TRENT**
Apprentice Editors . . . . **MIKE CUEVAS**
    JULIE ZUNDER, MARK GILLARD
Chief Lighting Technician . . . . . **DAVID DEVLIN**
Assistant Chief Lighting
    Technician . . . . . . **LARRY J. RICHARDSON**
Electricians . . . . **CHRIS BOTHWELL,**
    MAREK BOJSZA, GEOFFREY T. ENG,
    PAUL HAZARD, DAMON LIEBOWITZ,
    DAN McMAHON, DANIEL WINDELS
Rigging Gaffer . . . . **BRIAN R. LUKAS**
Rigging Best Boy . . . . **SCOT E. GAAL**
Key Grip . . . . **JIM KWIATKOWSKI**
Best Boy Grip . . . . **KEVIN ERB**
Dolly Grip . . . . **JERRY BERTOLAMI**
Grips . . . **JOHN MANG, ROBERT ANDERSON**
    ANTHONY CADY, JAMIE FRANTA,
    GREG HEWETT, WILLIS PIPKINS
Rigging Key Grip . . . . **CHARLEY H. GILLERAN**
Rigging Best Boy . . . . **KEVIN FAHEY**
Property Master . . . . **STEVEN B. MELTON**
Assistant Property Masters . . **LANCE LARSON,**
    GREGORY F. POULOS
    RITCHIE KREMER
Special Effects Coordinator . **JOHN HARTIGAN**
Special Effects Foreman . . **M. A. THOMPSON**
Special Effects Assistant . . . . **RON ROSEGARD**
Costume Supervisor **DEBORAH CHA BLEVINS**
Key Costumer . . . . **LORI DeLAPP**
Key Set Costumers . . . . **COOKIE LOPEZ**
    ANDREW SLYDER
Mr. Hanks' Costumer . . . **MARSHA BARTLETT**
Costumers . . . . **JENNY EAGAN,**
    ALIX HESTER, SUZANNE M. FLORES,
    CHRISTINE WADA, GUY MIRACLE,
    DIANA EDGMON, ANNIE GARRITY,
    ROBIN E. McMULLAN, MICHAEL LUTZ,
    APRIL KRUEGER, ANTHONY FRANCO,
    EMILY WYSS, JOSEPH REID
Cutter/Fitter . . . . **CELESTE CLEVELAND**
Tailor . . . . **PABLO NANTAS**
Department Head Makeup . . . **LOIS BURWELL**
Mr. DiCaprio's Makeup Artist . . . **SIÂN GRIGG**
Mr. Hanks' Makeup . . . **DANIEL C. STRIEPEKE**
Makeup Artists . . . . **LUISA ABEL,**
    DEBORAH LAMIA DENAVER
    MAGGIE E. ELLIOTT
Department Head
    Hair Stylist . . . . .**KATHRYN L. BLONDELL**
Key Hair Stylist . . . . **KIM SANTANTONIO**
Hair Stylists . . . . **AUDREY L. ANZURES**
    CAROLINE ELIAS, DOROTHY D. FOX
Production Supervisor . . . . **WILL WEISKE**
Production Coordinator . . . . **NELLIE ADAMI**

Assistant Production
    Coordinator . . . . **DEMELZA CRONIN**
Canada Supervisor . . . . **LILA YACOUB**
Special Projects . . . . **JOE BIGGINS**
Unit Supervisor . . . . **DAN COLLINS**
Production Associate . . **JENNIFER BARRONS**
Visual Effects Consultant **JOSEPH GROSSBERG**
Production Accountant . . . . **KELLY A. SNYDER**
First Assistant
    Accountant **LINDEN WINELAND-JOHNSON**
Second Assistant
    Accountants . . . . . . **JENNIFER L. CLARK**
    JAMES HINTON
Payroll Accountant . . . . **DANNY BOONE**
Construction Accountant . . **RENEÉ LEE ALITO**
Accounting Assistants . . . **GEORGE GOODWIN**
    NABUTILU KHALAYI
Associate
    to Mr. Spielberg . . . . . **KRISTIE MACOSKO**
Production Assistant
    to Mr. Spielberg . . . . **BEN BOHLING**
Assistants to Mr. Spielberg - LA . . **SUSAN RAY**
    ELIZABETH NYE
    KRIS KELLEY
Assistants to Mr. Parkes . . **LEILANI GUSHIKEN**
    JASON BIERFELD
Assistant to Ms. MacDonald . . . . **LINDA KROLL**
On-Set Assistant
    to Mr. DiCaprio . . . . **DAVID DiNOBLE**
Assistant to Mr. Hanks . . . . . . **AMY McKENZIE**
Location Manager . . . . **MIKE FANTASIA**
Assistant Location Managers **MADELINE BELL,**
    CHANEL CHADOCK, PETER COSTELLI,
    STEVEN S. LEE, DARRIN LIPSCOMB,
    DONNY MARTINO JR.
Location Scouts . . . . **LORI A. BALTON**
    RICHARD KLOTZ
Second Second
    Assistant Director . . . **JEFFREY SCHWARTZ**
Casting Assistant . . . . **ERIN TONER**
Extras Casting . . . . **SANDE ALESSI**
Extras Casting Associate . . **JENNIFER ALESSI**
Extras Casting Assistant . . . . . **SAGE ASTEAK**
Dialect Coach . . . . **JESSICA DRAKE**
Mr. DiCaprio's Dialect Consultant **TIM MONICH**
Unit Publicist . . . . **NANCY WILLEN**
Art Department Coordinator **FRANCINE BYRNE**
Set Designers . . . . **RANDALL WILKINS,**
    ANTHONY D. PARRILLO,
    SALLY THORNTON, SUZAN WEXLER
Graphics Designer . . . . . **MARTIN T. CHARLES**
Graphics . . . . **ADAM TANKELL**
Art Department Researcher . . . . . . **MAX DALY**
Art Department Production Assistants
    MELISSA BARTLEY, CIRCE MARINO
Clearance Coordinator . . . . **JODI TRIPI**
Clearance Assistant . . . . . **LUCA BORGHESE**
Buyers . **PAIGE AUGUSTINE, JOHN CAMPANA**
Set Decorator . . . . **CLAUDETTE DIDUL MANN**
Leadman . . . . **RUSS ANDERSON**
Drapery Foremen . . . . **BRAD CURRY**
    LAWRENCE D. LIRA
Draper . . . . **ABRAHAM VORSTER**
Swing Gang . . . . **DAVID MITCHELL,**
    STEVE PFAUTER, CURTIS ALLEN,
    JIMMY SIMEONE, E. SHEPHERD STEVENSON,
    ERIK POLCZWARTEK, CHANDLER VINAR,
    GENE TRAUTMANN, TIM BOWEN,
    RICK B. GLENN, TYLER KETTENBURG,
    JIM WARDELL, MICHAEL CASEY,
    BRENNER HUGH HARRIS, GREG BENGE
On Set Dresser . . . . **TROY PETERS**
Set Decoration Coordinator **RICHIE KAWAMOTO**
Construction Coordinator . **DAVE DEGAETANO**

General Foremen . . . . **STEVE RIGAMAT**
    JAVIER CARRILLO
Construction Foremen . . . . **VICTOR ESPINOZA,**
    RALPH J. FIERRO, CHUCK COBOS,
    RICARDO MONA, DARRYL ROBERTSHAW,
    BRETT HERNANDEZ, RUSSELL HURST
Labor Foremen . . **JOHN K. HILL, RICKIE GEE**
Tool Foreman . . . . **MIKE PAOLONE**
Plasterer Foreman . . . . **DAVID L. FALCONER**
Head Greensman . . . . **RANDY MARTENS**
Greens Foremen . . . . **JASON VANOVER**
    APRIL K. MARTENS
    STEVEN MARTINEZ
Paint Foremen . . . . **PAUL J. STANWYCK,**
    RICK BRODERMAN, BRETT A. TYLER,
    ROD GARVIN MICHAEL J. SMITH
Standby Painter . . . . **JOHN HINKLE**
Signwriter . . . . **JOHN L. ROOT**
Transportation Coordinator . . . . . **GENO HART**
Transportation Dispatcher . . . **STEVE LARSON**
Transportation Captain . . . . **JOE COSENTINO**
Transportation Co-Captains . . . **KIRK HUSTON**
    ANGEL DE SANTI
Picture Vehicle Coordinator . . . . **CYRIL O'NEIL**
Drivers . . . **TONY BARATTINI, MARK BASLER,**
    MICHAEL BELT, JODY BINGENHEIMER,
    CURTIS E. CLARK, PAT COSENTINO,
    SHERI LYNN COSENTINO, PAULIE DiCOCCO,
    DENNIS FAHEY, RICK FESE JR.,
    HECTOR M. GONZALEZ, DANIEL GORDON,
    DASH HART, STANLEY HOLMES,
    RON LINXWILER, MARCO LUPI,
    TED MEHOUS, J. LARRY MICHAEL,
    ESTEBAN MUÑOZ, BILL NEEDHAM,
    JAMES OBERMAN, DENNIS O'CONNELL,
    JOHN PELLEGRINO, JOHN SELLARS,
    STEVEN L. SHARE, CARLOS R. SOLANO,
    JOHN SPACCARELLI, SCOTT TYLER,
    ANTHONY JAMAL WADE, MARK WEBB,
    WILLIAM WEST, H. DAVE WILSON,
    ROBERT L. YOUNG JR.
Craft Service . . . . **GARY GINGOLD**
Craft Service Assistant . . . . **METI KUSARI**
Caterer . . . . **DELUXE CATERING**
Chef . . . . **JAMES FLEMMING**
FBI Technical Advisor . . . **WILLIAM J. REHDER**
Airplane Coordinator . . . . **BILL CASALE**
Dance Consultants . . . . . . **ADAM SHANKMAN,**
    ANNE FLETCHER
Teachers . . . . . . **LOIS CARL, RHODA C. FINE**
Production Assistants . . . . **KAYCE BROWN**
    BOBBIE BLYLE, AMANDA C. BROMBERG,
    CHRISTOPHER S. BRYSON,
    CESARE CALABRESE, KELLI CARDIFF,
    JERRY DIXON, KEITH DUNKERLEY,
    JEFFREY FOGLE JR., MARISA FORREST,
    ARIEL GOLD, MELISSA LEKUS,
    GREGORY J. PAWLIK JR.,
    NICHOLAS STANKEVICH,
    GEORGE DORIOAN THOMAS,
    GARY THOMAS WILLIAMS
On-Set Medic . . . . **THOMAS KRUEGER**
Construction Medics . . . . **HENRY HUMPHREYS**
    PAMELA CRUISE
Stand-in for Mr. DiCaprio . . . . **HUNTER CAZES**
Stand in for Mr. Hanks . . . . **ERIK FRYE**
Location Security . . . . **KEVIN BERMAN**
Security . . **ON SITE SECURITY, ERIC MEDINA**
Post Production Sound Facilities provided
by . . . . **TWENTIETH CENTURY FOX STUDIOS**
Supervising ADR Editor . . . . **R.J. KIZER**
Supervising Foley Editor . . . . **JOHN MURRAY**
First Assistant Sound Editor **DAVID A. WOLOWIC**

Assistant Sound Editor .... **BLAKE CORNETT**
Dialogue Editors .... **SUSAN DAWES**
MILDRED IATROU MORGAN
Sound Effects Editors .... **JOHN MORRIS**
TED CAPLAN
Re-Recordists .... **ROBERT RENGA**
CRAIG HEATH
Re-Recording Engineer .. **DENIS ST. AMAND**
ADR Mixer .... **CHARLEEN RICHARDS**
ADR Recordist .... **DAVID LUCARELLI**
ADR Voice Casting ...... **CAITLIN McKENNA**
Foley Artists ..... **ALICIA STEVENSON-IRWIN**
DAWN FINTOR
Foley Mixer .... **DAVID BETANCOURT**
Music Editor .... **KEN WANNBERG**
Assistant Music Editor ... **RAMIRO BELGARDT**
Orchestrations .... **JOHN NEUFELD**
Score Performed by .. **THE RECORDING ARTS**
ORCHESTRA OF LOS ANGELES
Featured Instrumentalists ....
Saxophone solos .... **DAN HIGGINS**
Vibraphone solos .... **ALAN ESTES**
Music Scoring Mixer .... **SHAWN MURPHY**
Music Preparation .... **JO ANN KANE**
MUSIC SERVICE
Orchestra Contractor .. **SANDY DECRESCENT**
Scoring Crew .... **SUE McLEAN**
MARK ESHELMAN, JASON LLOYD,
PATRICK WEBER, ADAM MICHALAK

Titles & Opticals .... **PACIFIC TITLE**
Negative Cutter .... **GARY BURRITT**
Color Timer .... **DALE GRAHN**
Camera Cranes & Dollies by
CHAPMAN/LEONARD STUDIO EQUIPMENT, INC.
Lighting by .... **PASKAL LIGHTING**

Head of FeatureProduction . **MICHAEL GRILLO**
Production Executive ..... **STEVEN R. MOLEN**
Executive Production
Coordinator .... **JENNIFER SANGER**
Post Production Executive .. **MARTIN COHEN**
Post Production Supervisor . **ERICA FRAUMAN**
Post Production
Coordinator .... **SVEN E.M. FAHLGREN**
Casting Executive .... **LESLEE FELDMAN**
Music Executive .... **TODD HOMME**
Production Controller .... **JIM TURNER**
Post Production Accountant ... **MARIA DeVANE**

NEW YORK CREW
Unit Production
Manager .. **MARI JO WINKLER-IOFFREDA**
Second Assistant Director .. **CHRISTO MORSE**
Art Director .... **PETER ROGNESS**
Assistant Art Director **MIGUEL LOPEZ-CASTILLO**
Set Decorator .... **ELAINE O'DONNELL**
Assistant Set Decorator ...... **KATE YATSKO**
B First Assistant Camera **ANDREW PRIESTLEY**
Sound Mixer .... **TERRANCE J. O'MARA**
Video Assist .... **MICHELLE MADER**
Chief Lighting Technician ..... **JIM RICHARDS**
Rigging Gaffer .... **GREG ADDISON**
Key Grip .... **THOMAS J. PRATE**
Dolly Grip .... **RONALD BURKE**
Key Rigging Grip .... **KENNETH J. BURKE**
Property Master .... **TOM McDERMOTT**
Special Effects Coordinator ... **CONNIE BRINK**
Assistant Costume Designer **LYNN P. HOFFMAN**
Costume Supervisors ..... **MICHAEL ADKINS**
PATRICIA A. EIBEN
Key Makeup .... **LINDA A. GRIMES**
Key Hair .... **MILTON BURAS**
Production Coordinator .... **JOHN DE SIMONE**

Assistant Production Coordinator **RAE UMSTED**
First Assistant
Accountant ... **OLIMPIA T. RINALDI-IODICE**
Payroll Accountant ..... **PATRICIA PORTER**
Location Manager ...... **ANDREW D. COOKE**
Assistant Location Manager **DAVID RAY MARTIN**
Location Scout .... **LYN PINEZICH**
Extras Casting .... **GRANT WILFLEY**
Art Department Coordinator ... **CLAIRE KIRK**
Leadman .... **PHIL CANFIELD**
Construction Coordinator ...... **NICK MILLER**
Charge Scenic .... **ROLAND BROOKS**
Transportation Captain ... **KEVIN K. KEEFE**
Transportation Co-Captains .. **JIM BUCKMAN**
JIMMY NUGENT
NY Picture Car Coordinator .... **JAMES MAHR**
Craft Service .... **CECIL B. DEMEALS**
Caterer .... **TOMKATS**

CANADA CREW
Unit Production Manager .... **RIC NISH**
Production Supervisor ...... **IRENE LITINSKY**
Second Assistant Director ... **BETHAN MOWAT**
Art Director .... **MICHÈLE LALIBERTÉ**
First Assistant Camera **CHRISTOPHER RAUCAMP**
Boom Operator/
Cable Person .... **NORMAN BERNARD**
Gaffer .... **JOHN LEWIN**
Key Rigging Gaffer .... **EAMES GAGNON**
Key Grips .... **ROBERT BRUCE BAYLIS**
ALAIN MASSÉ
Key Rigging Grip .... **STÉPHANE PILON**
Property Master .... **RÉAL BARIL**
Special Effects .... **L'INTRIGUE**
Special Effects Supervisor ..... **LOUIS CRAIG**
Wardrobe Coordinator ..... **DANIÈLE LÉGER**
Wardrobe Mistresses .... **JULIE GRAHAM**
MARIE-ÉTIENNE BESSETTE
Key Makeup .... **JOHANNE GRAVEL**
Key Hair .... **JOHANNE PAIEMENT**
Production Coordinator .... **DANIELLE LAVOIE**
Unit Manager .... **JEAN-YVES DOLBEC**
Assistant Unit Manager .. **PIERRE LAPOINTE**
Travel Coordinator **SANDRINE GROS D'AILLON**
Canada Production Accountant **BRUCE MILLER**
First Assistant Accountant .... **LUC BERNARD**
Assistant Accountant .... **BRENDA NIXON**
Payroll Accountant .... **RACHEL MANESS**
Location Manager .... **MICHÈLE ST-ARNAUD**
Assistant Location Managers **ALANA CYMERMAN**
CATHERINE LAVOIE
Montreal Casting Consultant **LUCIE ROBITAILLE**
Extras Casting .... **JULIE BRETON**
Set Designer .... **RUSSELL D. MOORE**
Decorators .... **PAUL HOTTE**
MARTINE KAZEMIRCHUK
Art Department Coordinator ... **DORIS SIMARD**
Construction Coordinator ... **MICHEL BROCHU**
Head Scenic Painter **VÉRONIQUE PAGNOUX**
Transportation Coordinator .... **JOSE URIA**
Driver Captain .... **RENÉ BRISSON**
Driver Co-Captain .... **JOSEPH VISCUSI**
Picture Vehicle Coordinator ..... **LUC POIRER**
Craft Service .... **GAÉTAN MERCIER**
Catering .... **ROCCO DE MONTREAL**
Production Services Provided by
MUSE ENTERTAINMENT ENTERPRISES INC.

Main Titles by
NEXUS PRODUCTIONS

Produced by .... **CHRIS O'REILLY** and
CHARLOTTE BAVASSO
2D Animation .... **AGNÈS FAUVE**
Layout & Typography ... **OLIVIER MARQUÉZY**

Editing .... **FLORENT PORTE**
3D Supervision .... **ROBIN KOBRYNSKI**
Visual Effects Supervision . **PATRICE MUGNIER**
3D & Compositing **PÉREGRINE MCCAFFERTY**
PIERRE SAVEL
2D Compositing ..... **PIERRE YVES JOSEPH**
Compositing
Assistance ...... **ALEXANDRE SCALVINO**
Production Co-Ordinator ..... **JULIA PARFITT**
Production Assistants ..... **JULIETTE STERN**
LUCY GLYN
Production Accountant **IAN MANSEL-THOMAS**

Visual Effects by
ASYLUM VISUAL EFFECTS

Sr. Visual Effects
Supervisor .... **NATHAN McGUINNESS**
Visual Effects Supervisor .... **MARC VARISCO**
Executive Producers ...... **BLONDEL AIDOO**
EMMA McGUINNESS
Visual Effects Producer ... **LINDSAY BURNETT**
CG Producer .... **JEFF WERNER**
Inferno Artists .... **TRAVIS BAUMANN,**
MITCH DRAIN, MARK RENTON,
ALEX ORTOLL, MARTY TAYLOR,
CANDICE SCOTT, PHIL BRENNAN
CG Artists .... **YUICHIRO YAMASHITA,**
MATHEW LAMB, MICHAEL HEMSCHOOT,
JASON SHUGARDT
Matte Paintings ...... **ROBERT STROMBERG**
2D Artists .... **PATRICK KAVANAUGH,**
BRANDON CRISWELL, JOE KEN
Visual Effects Editor . **KRISTOPHER KASPER**
Asst. Visual Effects Editor **ZACHARY JUSTMAN**
Engineering .... **BILL LAVERTY,**
ALEX HEGEDUS
Head of Technology .... **TOMMY HOOPER**
I/O ....**BRIAN CUSCINO, GREG MUCINO**
Video .... **LEE ROBINSON**
Consultant .... **FRANK W. ABAGNALE**

The Producers Wish To Thank:
The California Film Commission
Entertainment Industry Development Corporation
City of Los Angeles Department of Transportation
Los Angeles World Airports
The New York Mayor's Office of Film,
Theater and Broadcasting
New York City Police Department Traffic
Intelligence Unit
New York City General Services Administration
New York State Governor's Office
for Motion Picture and Television
New York Metropolitan Transit Authority
New Jersey Motion Picture and
Television Commission
The Port Authority of New York and New Jersey
New Jersey Transit
HSBC Bank USA
The Quebec City Film Commission
SODEC
Thanks to Riverbend Apartments and Julian
LeCraw & Co., Inc. Atlanta, Georgia

The Residents of the cities of Los Angeles,
Pasadena, Downey, Santa Ana, Pomona,
Ontario, Burbank, Redondo Beach, Altadena,
and Compton, CA; New York City, Yonkers, NY
and Orange, NJ; and Montreal and Quebec
City whose consideration and cooperation
enabled us to make this film.

"To Tell The Truth" courtesy of Fremantle Media

"Warren Commission" courtesy of
NBC News Archives

"Dragnet" courtesy of Universal
Studios Licensing LLP

Jack Webb™ Licensed by
The Roger Richman Agency, Inc.

"Goldfinger" courtesy of MGM Clip and Still

"Dr. Kildare" courtesy of Turner Entertainment Co.

Scene from "The Odd Couple"
courtesy of Paramount Pictures

"Perry Mason" courtesy of CBS Broadcasting Inc.

"The Flash" comic books provided by DC Comics

SONGS

TO TELL THE TRUTH
Written by Paul Alter & Robert Israel

EMBRACEABLE YOU
Words & Music by George Gershwin & Ira Gershwin
Performed by Judy Garland, Courtesy of MCA
Records, Under license from Universal Music
Enterprises

PUT YOUR HEAD ON MY SHOULDER
Written by Paul Anka, Performed by The
Lettermen, Courtesy of Capitol Records
Under license from EMI Film & Television Music

BODY & SOUL
Written by John Green, Edward Heyman,
Robert Sour & Frank Eyton, Performed by Erroll
Garner, Courtesy of SLG, LLC

I'VE GOT THE WORLD ON A STRING
Written by Harold Arlen & Ted Koehler
Performed by Teddy Wilson, Milt Hinton &
Oliver Jackson, Courtesy of LRC Ltd.

TAKE THE A TRAIN
Written by Billy Strayhorn

THE GIRL FROM IPANEMA
Written by Antonio Carlos Jobim & Vinicius De
Moraes, English lyrics by Norman Gimbel,
Performed by Stan Getz & Joao Gilberto,
featuring Antonio Carlos Jobim, Courtesy of
The Verve Music Group Under license from
Universal Music Enterprises

THE JAMES BOND THEME
Written by Monty Norman, Performed by Prague
Philharmonic Orchestra, Courtesy of Silva America

THE LOOK OF LOVE
Written by Burt Bacharach & Hal David
Performed by Dusty Springfield, Courtesy of
Mercury Records, Under license from Universal
Music Enterprises

MELE KALIKIMAKA
Written by Alex Anderson, Performed by Bing
Crosby, Courtesy of MCA Records, Under
license from Universal Music Enterprises

HE'S SO FINE
Written by Ronald Mack, Performed by
The Chiffons, Courtesy of Capitol Records
Under license from EMI Film & Television Music

YOU REALLY GOT ME
Written by Ray Davies, Performed by The Kinks
Courtesy of Sanctuary Records Group

UN POCO ADAGIO
from Piano Concerto No. 11 in D, Performed by
Leif Ove Andsnes & The Norwegian Chamber
Orchestra, Courtesy of EMI Classics
Under license from EMI Film & Television Music

HAS ANYBODY HERE SEEN KELLY?
Written by C.W. Murphy, William McKenna,
& John Charles Moore
Performed by The Mitch Miller Singers

THE WAY YOU LOOK TONIGHT
Written by Dorothy Fields & Jerome Kern
Performed by The Lettermen, Courtesy of
Capitol Records, Under license from EMI Film
& Television Music

I'LL BE HOME FOR CHRISTMAS
Written by Walter Kent, Kim Gannon & Buck Ram
Performed by The Hollyridge Strings, Courtesy
of Capitol Records, Under license from
EMI Film & Television Music

I CAN'T GIVE YOU ANYTHING BUT LOVE
Written by Dorothy Fields & Jimmy McHugh
I'M SHOOTING HIGH
Written by Ted Koehler & Jimmy McHugh
Performed by Ellis Hall & BeB'Opera

LEAVING ON A JET PLANE
Written by John Denver

COME FLY WITH ME
Written by Sammy Cahn & James Van Heusen
Performed by Frank Sinatra, Courtesy of Capitol
Records, Under license from EMI Film &
Television Music

LES ANGES DANES NOS CAMPAGNES
Peuple Fideles, Arranged by Gregory Charles

THE CHRISTMAS SONG
Written by Mel Torme & Robert Wells
Performed by Nat King Cole, Courtesy of Capitol
Records, Under license from EMI Film &
Television Music

Soundtrack on **DREAMWORKS RECORDS**

Filmed with
PANAVISION® CAMERAS & LENSES

Edited on the Moviola™
Prints by Technicolor® Kodak
Dolby™ Digital, In Selected Theatres
DTS™ Sound, In Selected Theatres
SDDS Sony Dynamic Digital Sound,
In Selected Theatres

MPAA # 39409
I.A.T.S.E.

**Copyright © 2002 DREAMWORKS LLC
All Rights Reserved.**

DreamWorks LLC is the author and creator of this
motion picture for purposes of the berne convention
and all national laws giving effect thereto, and for
purposes of copyright law in the united kingdom.

While this picture is based upon a true story, many
characters are composites or inventions, and a number of incidents fictionalized.

This motion picture is protected under the laws of
the united states and other countries. Unauthorized
duplication, distribution or exhibition may result in
civil liability and criminal prosecution.

Distributed by
**DREAMWORKS DISTRIBUTION LLC
DREAMWORKS PICTURES
AMBLIN**

*Credits not final.

A special thank you to this book's many contribu-
tors—particularly Frank W. Abagnale — for
their time, information, and words. An additional
thanks to the following at DreamWorks for their
invaluable contributions:

Corinne Antoniades
Melissa Baldwin
Kristy Cox
Paul Elliott
Anne Globe
Mike Gottberg
Leilani Gushiken
Marvin Levy
Rhion Magee
Boyd Peterson
Susan Ray
Dorit Saines
David Sameth
Jennifer Sanger
Daniel Yankelevits

BT 505057
22.95
5/22/03

ABOVE: Director Steven Spielberg (center, in parka) with the crew of Catch Me If You Can.

Now read the book upon which the movie is based.

Frank W. Abagnale, alias Frank Williams, Robert Conrad, Frank Adams, and Robert Monjo, was one of the most daring con men, forgers, imposters, and escape artists in history. Now recognized as the nation's leading authority on financial foul play, Abagnale is a charming rogue whose hilarious, stranger-than-fiction international escapades and ingenious escapes — including one from an airplane — make *Catch Me If You Can* an irresistible tale of deceit.

"A book that captivates from first page to last." —*WEST COAST REVIEW OF BOOKS*

"Zingingly told...richly detailed and winning as the devil." —*KIRKUS REVIEWS*

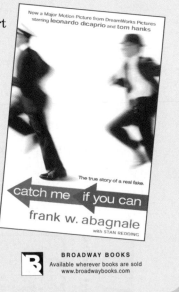

BROADWAY BOOKS
Available wherever books are sold
www.broadwaybooks.com